AT LAST! THE OFFICIAL IRISH JOKE BOOK NO. 2

Also in this series:

KEVIN MURTIE

AT LAST! THE OFFICIAL IRISH JOKE BOOK NO. 2

Futura

A Futura Book

First published in Great Britain in 1985 by
Futura Publications, a Division of
Macdonald & Co (Publishers) Ltd
London & Sydney
Reprinted 1989

ISBN 0 7088 2669 5

Photoset in North Wales by
Derek Doyle & Associates, Mold, Clwyd
Printed in Great Britain by
BPCC Hazell Books Ltd
Member of BPCC Ltd
Aylesbury, Bucks, England

Futura Publications
A Division of
Macdonald & Co (Publishers) Ltd
66–73 Shoe Lane
London EC4P 4AB
A member of Maxwell Pergamon Publishing Corporation plc

An oil rig in the desert went up in flames, and the Arabs sent for Red Adair to put the fire out. While they were waiting for him to arrive, an old battered van raced onto the scene and went straight into the midst of the smoke and flames.

Half a dozen Irishmen jumped out and started battering the flames out with old coats and wellies. Half an hour later the fire was completely extinguished, and the grateful Arabs gave the men £100,000 to share among themselves.

'Thanks a lot,' said the driver. 'The first thing I'll do is to get my brakes mended.'

Heard in a Wicklow post office: 'I always get my stamps at the counter-they're fresher than the machine.'

An Irish rugby fan, staying in London for a big match, phoned the hotel receptionist to complain he couldn't find the zip in his sleeping bag.
'There's not a zip,' she retorted. 'It's a duvet.'

Poodle: 'Do you have a family tree?'
Irish wolfhound: 'No, we ain't particular.'

Galway police today arrested a camper and charged him with loitering within tent. – *News item.*

Then there was the Belfast man charged with parking his car on a double yellow line. As he explained in court, the sign said 'Fine for parking' so he did.

☆

What about the Larne girl who washed down the pill with pond water? Three months later she was stagnant.

☆

A Belfast woman and her small boy were passed by two nuns in a Dublin street. The boy asked: 'What d'ye call them, ma?'
'For Gawd's sake,' she rebuked him, 'houl yer tongue or they'll know we're not one of them.'

☆

A sign at Runnymeade read: 'Magna Carta signed here 12.15.'
'Drat it,' the Irish tourist said to his wife, 'we've missed it by twenty minutes.'

☆

What about the Cork man who painted his house during the height of summer, bundled up to the ears? As he explained, it said on the tin to be sure to put on three coats.

☆

Notice in a Letterkenny pet shop: 'In the interest of dogs, hygiene is not permitted in this shop.'

☆

A guest house owner in Bray was 'phoned with a request for a room with a bath and toilet.
'I'm sorry we haven't a room with a toilet,' she replied, 'but I can let you have one overlooking the sea.'

Notice at Galway undertakers: 'Parking for clients only.'

After reading the *Penguin Book of Quotations*, Patrick remarked that he didn't realise penguins had so much to say.

'What time does the hotel bar open, Miss?'
'Five o'clock – but you can have a drink while you're waiting.'

Then there was the Irish tree surgeon who fell out of his patient.

'Would you like the soap scented or unscented, madam?'
'Oi t'ink oi'l take it with me.'

What about the Irishman who was asked by the doctor to stand on one foot? He stood on the doctor's.

Following a two-year study by typewriting experts, it was announced today that the Irish Doomsday Book is a forgery. – *News item*.

☆

'Rooms with a sea view at this hotel are thirty pounds a day, Mr O'Toole.'
'How much if oi promise not to look?'

☆

Irishman to Englishman: 'I've never played darts on a dartboard, but I'll give you a game for a tenner.'
'Right,' said the Englishman, 'you're on.'
The Irishman started with 180, then went on to win the game in record time.
'Come on,' said the Englishman, 'I thought you said you hadn't played on a dartboard before?'
'Neither I have,' replied the Irishman, 'but I used to practise on flies crawling up the wall.'
'Didn't it make a mess of the wallpaper?'
'Not at all ... I used to pin them by their legs.'

☆

Then there was the Cork man who paid for his holiday on HP. He reasoned that if the plane crashed he'd get a free holiday.

☆

Hard luck on the Irish Humpty Dumpty – the wall fell on top of him.

☆

Did you hear about the Irish comedian who walked off stage in the middle of his act? He complained that everyone was laughing at him.

☆

Tourist: 'How far is it to Waterford, Pat?'
'How did you know my name?'
'I guessed it.'
'Then guess how far it is to Waterford.'

☆

The stage director called the Irish actor over.
'Listen,' he said, 'you're the stand-in so you're supposed to be dressed exactly the same as the star. Why are you wearing wellingtons?'
'Well, you see,' came the reply, 'I don't know what I've got to stand in.'

☆

Notice in Dublin doctor's waiting-room: 'Will patients please not exchange symptoms as this confuses the doctor.'

☆

'A packet of cigarettes, please.'
'Ten or twenty?'
'Twenty.'
'Turkish or Virginian?'
'Virginian.'
'Cork tipped or plain?'
'Cork tipped.'
'Soft pack or hard pack?'
'Forget it — I've packed up smoking.'

☆

Finbarr went to the doctor with steering wheel trouble. As he explained, 'I keep getting these awful turns.'

☆

Lot 74 One pair unique 17th century silver candlesticks.
Lot 75 Another pair, ditto. — *From an Irish auctioneer's catalogue.*

☆

'You say your wife covers her face with raspberry yoghurt every night, Sean? Is it beneficial?'
'Well, it helps ... but I can still see it's her.'

☆

Notice at a market at Newtonards: Leo Tard's, £1.25.

☆

Then there was the Irishman on *What's My Line?* who was asked to give the panel a clue.
'I'm in marine and agriculture,' he told them.
When the panel gave up, he explained that he owned a fish-and-chip shop.

☆

Sign on a battered jalopy in Belfast: 'It's the way I crash 'em.'

☆

As the Irishman said while watching Torvill and Dean on TV: 'Those cameramen must be good skaters to follow the dancers so well.'

☆

'What's that t'ing in the garden?'
'It's a bird-bath.'
'You're puttin' me on.'
'No – honest. Why the surprise?'
'Sure, I just don't believe birds can tell when it's Saturday night.'

☆

Two Irishmen got talking at an Orange Walk. 'Tell me,' said one, 'which part of the North are you from?'
'Actually,' said the other, 'I'm from Cork.'
'Really? And when do you walk?'
'When the bus fares go up.'

☆

It could only happen in Ireland. At a soccer match the players swopped jerseys at half-time.

☆

Graffiti: IRISH SAMARITANS DO IT EX-DIRECTORY.

☆

Note to milkman in Donegal: 'No milk today. By today I mean tomorrow as I wrote this yesterday.'

☆

Farmer: 'You must be brave to come down by parachute in this gale.'
Brendan: 'I didn't come down by parachute, I went up in a tent.'

☆

'Whisper something soft and sweet in my ear, Michael.'
'Black Forest cherry cake.'

☆

Patrick to boss: 'I'm a pound short this week.'
'You didn't say anything last week when you were paid a pound too much.'
'I know – I can overlook one mistake, but when it happens twice ...'

☆

Why does it take ten Irishmen to change a light bulb?
One to fit it and nine to move the room round.

☆

Teacher: 'What do you know about Kipling, Bridget?'
Pupil: 'Please, miss, he makes exceedingly good cakes.'

☆

Notice on a shop in Belfast: Closed for altercations.

☆

Billy Connolly (to noisy hecklers in Dublin): 'Hey, put the house lights on. I want tae *see* an Irish joke.'

☆

'Television?' said O'Reilly. 'We switch it off more than we switch it on.'

☆

Did you hear about the Cork man who had a brain transplant? The brain rejected him.

☆

Plans are afoot to build a Post Office tower in Connemara. The restaurant will stand still while the diners run round in circles.

☆

Why do Irish undertakers go to Wembley? For the Hearse of the Year Show.

☆

Two out-of-work Irishmen were walking past Jodrell Bank.
'Let's try here for work,' suggested one.
'Not on your life,' replied the other. 'Look at the size of that cement mixer.'

☆

'Do you sell loose cigarettes?'
'Yes, we do. How many do you want?'
'Give us twenty.'

☆

Brendan found a wage packet in the street. 'You're dead lucky, so you are,' said his pal.
'Lucky?' said Brendan. 'Look at the tax I've paid!'

☆

'Tell me, Michael, where does the Queen sit at a Royal Variety Performance?'
'Sure, she has her own royal box.'
'You'd t'ink they'd give her a proper seat, wouldn't you?'

☆

Did you hear about the Irishman who ran away with a circus? The police caught him and made him bring it back.

'Hello, is that the Dublin asylum?'
'Yes, but we're not on the phone.'

Then there was the pregnant woman in Belfast who asked her doctor: 'Will I have a sectarian birth?'

O'Shaughnessy was charged with stealing cars. He was told by the judge he could either be tried by his peers, or dealt with by him alone.
'What do you mean by peers?' O'Shaughnessy asked.
'Peers are your equals, men of your own class and kind,' the judge replied.
'In that case,' said O'Shaughnessy, 'I'd rather be judged by you alone. I certainly don't want to be tried by a bunch of car thieves.'

Murphy put a parcel on the bar. 'What's that?' asked the barman.
'It's my lunch,' said Murphy.
'Is it ticking?'
'No – it's turkey.'

Irish raider in Chinese restaurant: 'All the money in the till.'

Chinaman: 'To take away?'

☆

Seamus was killed in a car accident and arrived at the Pearly Gates. 'Are you a Jehovah's Witness?' asked St Peter.

'To tell you the truth,' replied Seamus, 'it all happened so quickly I didn't even see the accident.'

☆

Notice in a Limerick Hotel: 'Please do not turn on TV except when in use.'

☆

A man phoned the tourist office and asked the cost of a room at a Malahide hotel. 'Sorry,' he was told, 'the brochure with the details isn't out yet.'

'When do you expect it?'

'I really don't know.'

'The hotel isn't in the phone book. Should I ring directory enquiries?'

'I've no idea.'

'You don't mind me asking all these questions?'

'Not at all – sure, that's what we're here for.'

☆

What's so special about Irish Radio? It has sub-titles for the deaf.

☆

Irishman in baker's: 'I want to know who's been signing my name on your Hot Cross buns.'

A mistake was made in the Christian name of a man accused of a motoring offence in Cork. He decided not to go to court, but arranged for his brother to be there to see what happened.

When the offender's name was called out, a shout came from the gallery: 'There's no such man.'

'Then who are you?' asked the clerk.

'Sure, I'm his brother.'

Michael in record shop: 'Do you have *Rhapsody in Blue*?'

'Sorry, sir, it's out of stock.'

'Then perhaps you have it in some other colour?'

Then did you hear about the Irish dyslexic who asked at his local library for George Orwell's *1948*?

Insurance agent: 'This is a particularly good policy, Mrs O'Gorman. Under it, we pay £5000 for broken arms and legs.'

'Glory be … what do you do with them all?'

Tough luck on the Irish astronauts. When they tried to land on the Moon it was full.

Did you hear about the Linfield goalkeeper who was nicknamed Cinderella? He kept missing the ball.

A five-year-old Cork boy coming home from school in tears, explained that the teacher had asked all those who wanted to go to heaven to raise their hands.

'You raised yours, didn't you?' asked his mother.

'No,' sobbed the boy, 'you told me to be sure to come straight home.'

☆

Irish sports commentator: 'And now over for hearse racing at Horst Park.'

☆

'Stop playin',' Patrick said, interrupting the card game, 'Mulligan is cheating.'

'How do you make that out?' asked Mulligan.

'You're not playin' the hand I dealt you with.'

☆

Why, wondered Murphy, do all the big stores have sales when everywhere's packed out with folk? Sure, it'd be better altogether if they waited until things got quieter.

☆

For sale: Austin 1972 hearse. Body in good condition. — *Belfast Telegraph.*

☆

'I noticed all your chickens out in the front garden yesterday, Brendan.'

'Yes, they heard that men were going to lay the pavement and they wanted to see how it was done.'

☆

17

Did you hear about the one-fingered Irish pickpocket?
He only stole Polo Mints.

☆

'How did you get those scars on top of your nose, Eamonn?'
'Sure, I got them from glasses.'
'Why don't you try contact lenses?'
'Ah, well, they don't hold enough beer.'

☆

Then there was the Irishman who called at the Blood Bank – and asked for two pints.

☆

Priest: 'Are you troubled with indecent thoughts, Mary?'
Mary: 'To tell you the truth, Father, I quite enjoy them.'

☆

Spare a thought for the Irish electrician who found shorts in his wife's bedroom.

☆

Michael saw an advert for a body-building book and sent away for it. Three months later he wrote to the publishers: 'I've read your book now. Please send muscles by return.'

☆

Graffiti: 'IF YOU FEEL STRONGLY ABOUT TOILET GRAFFITI, SIGN A PARTITION.'

☆

Did you hear about the Killarney boy who was warned not to go into the water immediately after lunch as it was dangerous to swim on a full stomach? He swam on his back.

☆

Wife:'That was some thunderstorm we had last night, Sean.'
'Why didn't you wake me up? You know I can't sleep in a thunderstorm.'

☆

Then there was the Irish poultry farmer who went broke giving away free range eggs.

☆

Journalists were being given an outline of the Irish team's tactical plan at the next World Cup.
'Our whole idea,' they were told, 'is to equalise before the other team scores.'

☆

'Off to school now,' said Noreen's mother, 'and don't speak to strangers unless you know them.'

☆

Car sticker: HELP A NUN KICK THE HABIT.

☆

Did you hear about the Irish test tube baby? Every Father's Day he puts a bunch of flowers in the fridge.

☆

'Give me a sentence with the word bewitches in it.'
'Go on ahead and I'll bewitches in a minute.'

☆

What about the man going to see *Jaws III* at a Dublin cinema? He asked for a seat in the shallow end.

☆

Policeman: 'I'm going to throw the book at you. No lights, two bald tyres, no number plates, no windscreen wipers, no indicators …'
Seamus to pal: 'I told you this car wasn't worth pinching.'

☆

Notice in a lift in Cork: 'Eighth floor button out of order. Please push buttons five and three.'

☆

Then there was the Irish tramp charged in court with stealing a bottle of perfume. He was convicted of fragrancy.

☆

'Perhaps you can tell the court how you can possibly justify breaking into the same house three times in one week?'
'I put it down to the housing shortage, your honour.'

☆

Why do Irish policemen always go around in threes?
So there's one who can read, one who can make phone calls, and one to keep an eye on the two intellectuals.

☆

Notice in the window of a Belfast rental shop: 'Life membership – for a limited period only.'

☆

A man helped a nun across a busy road? 'Thank you very much,' she said.
'Not at all,' came the reply. 'Any friend of Batman is a friend of mine.'

☆

'Have you seen what's going on in Cambodia?'
'I can't see a thing where we are – we live at the back.'

☆

Sign in Co. Kildare: Self-service undertaker.

☆

Did you hear about the Irishman in Saudi Arabia who drank a bottle of whiskey and got fifty lashes? In that country, you take your drinks first and have a whip-round later.

☆

'Is that Dublin double two double two?'
'No, this is Dublin two two two two.'
'Oh, sorry to have bothered you.'
'That's all right – the phone was ringing anyway.'

☆

21

Mean? Did you hear about the Howth golfer who got a hole in one? In the bar afterwards he denied it.

☆

Lost, tabby cat, male, answers to Jim. Reward (one black eye). — *Irish paper.*

☆

Then there was the Cork man who thought St Michael was the patron saint of underwear.

☆

'Dad, I flunked the geography test. I forgot where the Himalayas were.'
'I've told you a thousand times — try and remember where you put things.'

☆

What about the Belfast night club that employed a chucker-in?

☆

'Ma, what's a bazooka?'
'It's a kind of military weapon.'
'Well, Sean's got one on his foot.'

☆

O'Casey: 'How's your wife?'
Murphy: 'Compared to what?'

☆

Michael wasn't all that keen to take severance pay till he knew what they were going to sever.

Wife to tramp: 'You know, you'd stand a better chance of a job if you shaved, had a haircut, and cleaned yourself up.'

'Yes, Ma'am, I found that out years ago.'

☆

Did you hear about the Irish hammer thrower at the Olympics who was given a dope test? He passed.

☆

Notice in a Dublin dress shop: 'Wedding gowns for all occasions.'

☆

An Irishman with no legs was sitting in a pub at closing time.

'Are you waiting for someone, Paddy?' asked the barman.

'Aye,' replied Paddy. 'A carry out.'

☆

Clancy was driving along in his car with a hitchhiker. Without stopping, he went straight through a red light.

'Why didn't you stop?' asked the hitchhiker.

'Well,' explained Clancy, 'my brother never stops for a red light, and he's never had an accident.'

He drove through two more red lights. As he was approaching the fourth, the lights changed to green ... and Clancy came to a screeching halt.

'Why did you stop at the green light?' asked the hitchhiker.

'Simple,' replied Clancy. 'My brother could be coming the other way, and as I told you, he doesn't stop for red lights.'

☆

Tim was stopped for drunken driving. The policeman handed him a balloon and told him to blow it up.

'Very well,' said Tim, 'who's in goal?'

☆

Spare a thought for the Irish MENSA Society. He fell downstairs and broke a leg.

☆

As the pilot of a plane was about to take off from an airfield in Galway, he was handed a weather forecast.

'But this is five years old,' he complained.

'I know,' replied the met. officer, 'but, sure, the weather here never changes.'

☆

Did you hear about the Irishman in Israel who was living the life of Cohen?

☆

'Doctor, you remember last year you told me to stay away from dampness if I wanted my rheumatism to get better?'

'Indeed I do.'

'Well, now it's better is it all right for me to take a bath?'

News flash: In the international relay at the White City today, the Irish team built up a commanding lead before handing the baton to the East German team.

Driving in the country, Finbarr saw a sign: BEWARE OF SHEEP. 'Well, I never,' he remarked to his wife, 'I didn't know they were dangerous.'

☆

A patient in a private hospital in Dublin complained about the anaesthetist's charge. 'Two hundred pounds just to put me to sleep?' she asked.
'No,' replied the nurse, 'It's to be sure you wake up again.'

☆

Patrick came up with an idea to strengthen Sterling.
– Add starch to all one pound notes.

☆

Sign in Kilkenny bar: 'Stay a little longer. Your wife can only get *so* mad.'

☆

What about the Irish entertainer who does impressions with a difference? Nobody recognises them.

☆

'Was your husband's funeral expensive, Mrs Muldoon?'
'Indeed it was. Sure, for the past three years, it's cost me sixty pounds a week.'
'Whyever's that?'
'Well, you see, I buried him in a Moss Bros suit.'

☆

25

One Irishman bet another a thousand pounds he couldn't carry him across Niagara Falls on a tightrope. After a hair-raising trip, they finally made it to the other side.

Handing over the money, Brendan said, 'You know, I was sure I'd won the bet when you wobbled half-way over.'

☆

What is Irish matched luggage? Two plastic shopping bags from Marks and Spencer.

☆

A delivery man called at O'Reilly's house. 'Who is it?' asked O'Reilly.

'It's the Venetian blind,' came the reply.

'Go away,' he shouted. 'I gave you a donation last week.'

☆

On holiday in Canada, O'Shaughnessy came across a sign saying 'Bear to the right, ... so he turned left.

☆

An Irish firm offered work in a prune-tasting factory. 'Good opportunity – work one day, off three.'

☆

What about the awkward Irishman in a bar: 'Single Diamond, please.'

☆

Magnus: 'Who wrote Ravel's Bolero?'
Irishman: 'Pass.'

Patrick went to buy travellers cheques for his holiday abroad.
'What denomination?' asked the clerk.
'Church of Ireland,' he replied.

Then there was the Cork man who went big-game hunting in Africa. He bagged a lion ... and bagged and bagged it to go away.

Clancy staggered out of the pub and had got into his car, when a policeman came over. 'You're not thinking of driving, are you?' the officer asked.
'To tell you the truth,' replied Clancy, 'I'm in no condition to walk.'

☆

What about the Irishman, invited to a conference on schizophrenia, who had half a mind to attend?

☆

A Scotsman, an Englishman and an Irishman were up before a firing squad. Noticing how nervous the squad were, they hit upon the idea of giving them a sudden shock to put them off their stroke.
'Flood!' yelled the Scotsman, and the soldiers dropped their rifles and ran away.
'Earthquake!' shouted the Englishman, and again the soldiers fled.
Then it was the Irishman's turn. '*Fire!*' he yelled.

An impresario was passing a building site when he saw a workman do three double somersaults, a jack-knife, a back flip, and land on his feet.

Rushing up to him, the impresario said: 'I'll book you for *Live From Her Majesty's.*'

'In that case,' said the foreman, 'you'd better book big Paddy, too. He's the feller that hit him with the sledgehammer.'

☆

What about the Belfast man who drinks whiskey and Horlicks? When it's his turn to buy a round he's asleep.

☆

Trust an Irish housewife to make chips with *Smash.*

☆

An Irishman went to the doctor and said he was not gaining any weight.

'What do you have for breakfast?' asked the doctor.

'Snooker balls,' came the reply. 'Three reds, two blues and a brown.'

'How about dinner?'

'Two blacks, three yellows and a red.'

'I can see your problem,' said the doctor. 'You're not getting enough greens.'

☆

Did you hear about the Killarney golfer whose ball lodged in an enormous oak? He got it out with a tree iron.

☆

'Is your wife jealous?'
'Jealous? She won't even let the priest in because he wears a skirt.'

Sad news about Sean. He was born stupid, and now he's had a relapse.

Keen but out-of-work actor seeks non-appearing, non-speaking parts. – *Irish Times*.

Notice outside a Dublin church: 'Genesis is Good for You.'

A tourist ran over a White Leghorn hen near O'Grady's farm. He picked up the bird and called in to apologise.
'What makes you think the hen is mine?' asked O'Grady.
'Well, you raise White Leghorns, don't you?'
'Yes,' agreed O'Grady, 'but not flat ones like that.'

Two Irishmen were watching TV.
One said: 'Which side was the Pope shot on?'
'I think it was ITV,' the other replied.

'I hope you don't mind me mentioning it, Mrs Grogan, but your daughter's busy knitting baby clothes.'
'Ah, well, anything to take her mind off boys.'

Then there was the Irishman who got tennis elbow playing tiddlewinks.

Eamonn lost his Army rifle. The sergeant said: 'You'll have to pay for it.'
'That's ridiculous,' said Eamonn. 'What would you do if I lost a tank?'
'You'd have to pay for that, too.'
'No wonder Navy captains go down with their ships.'

A dangerous criminal escaped from Broadmoor, so the police issued photographs showing his left profile, front view and right profile.
A few days later, they received a message from an Irish detective:
'Have captured the fellow on the left, and the fellow in the middle. At this rate, it won't be long before I catch the fellow on the right as well.'

Bridget: 'Doctor, even though I've been on the pill, I'm pregnant. Shall I keep on taking it?'
'Yes, but double the quantity. Remember, you're taking it for two now.'

Wife: 'A fine time to come home. I want an explanation and I want the truth.'
Michael: 'Make up your flippin' mind.'

Then there was the Irishman who looked up his family tree and found half the family were still living in it.

☆

Graffiti: KEEP THE BOAT PEOPLE OUT – SINK THE IRISH FERRY.

☆

'The world title fight in Belfast was stopped in the 11th round tonight to save the ref from further punishment.' – *News flash*.

☆

The rugby match between the Archbishop's XV and the Pope's XV ended in a draw. The Archbishop's team got all the tries and the Pope's XV made all the conversions.

☆

Why did the Irish hedgehog cross the road? To find his flatmate.

☆

Christopher was at a football match.
At regular intervals he took a can of beer from a bag and laboriously opened each with a tin-opener, being careful not to spill any.
A spectator next to him was intrigued. 'Why don't you just open the cans with the ring-pull?' he asked.
'Oh,' said Christopher, 'I thought that was just for people who forgot their tin-openers.'

☆

Did you hear about the Killarney group who called themselves Instant Potato? They were hoping for a Smash hit.

☆

Announcement on Irish TV: 'We must apologise for a fault in the programme about compost heaps. The programme will continue in smell only.'

☆

'Is that hand knitted?'
'No – it came with my arms.'

☆

What about the Cork man who returned a Louis XIV bed because it was too small, and asked for a Louis XV?

☆

Sean was taken to his first cricket match. Whilst he was watching, the batsman hit a six, three fours, and two singles.
'That bowler's very good,' he remarked. 'No matter where the batsman puts his bat, he manages to hit it.'

Notice in Co. Wicklow: 'Beware! To touch these wires is instant death. Anyone found doing so will be prosecuted.'

☆

Patrick was about to land on an airfield when his passenger reminded him that he was piloting a seaplane. So Patrick flew to the nearest stretch of water and made a perfect landing.

'Thanks very much for reminding me,' he said ... and stepped out of the plane into the water.

☆

A shame about Brian's shock-proof, waterproof watch. It caught fire.

☆

'Could oi have some pate, please?'

'Certainly, sir. Which kind of pate would you like?'

'Pate for puttin' glass in windows.'

☆

Returning home after a lengthy pub crawl, Murphy asked his wife: 'Is my meal warm?'

'If it is,' she replied, 'the dustbin's on fire.'

☆

Trust an Irishman to come up with a new plan for the Channel Tunnel. As soon as it's built, fill it with water. Then passengers will be able to get through it on the cross-Channel ferry.

☆

Heard at Dublin Airport: 'The Aer Lingus flight to London will depart when the little hand is on the nine and the big hand is on the five.'

☆

'I'm givin' up the fiddle, Mike, and learnin' to play the piano.'
'Why's that?'
'Sure, my Guinness keeps slidin' off the fiddle.'

Spotted in Liverpool: an Indian takeaway, a Chinese takeaway, and an Irish bring-it-back.

'That's a lovely suit you're wearing, Brendan.'
'Yes, it was a surprise present from the missus.'
'A surprise, was it?'
'Indeed it was. I came home early one night and found it lying on the bed.'

Then there was the Irishman who went to the doctor for more sleeping pills for his wife. She'd woken up.

Poster outside the Army recruiting office in Cork: 'The Army will make you a man.' Bridget went in and put down a deposit for two.

'Do you always drink your whiskey neat, Eamonn?'
'No – sometimes I drink it with no tie on and my shirt hanging out.'

What about the Irish long-distance lorry driver who landed a job on the Isle of Man?

☆

And the Irish pigeon that put everything it had on Lester Piggott?

☆

An Irish soldier tried to convince his Commanding Officer that he was no good for the Army. 'I'm bad with nerves,' he said. 'If anybody shouts at me, I jump.'
The C.O. transferred him to the Paratroopers.

☆

You could tell Maureen had been an ice-cream seller in a cinema before her wedding – she walked down the aisle backwards.

☆

And did you hear about the Portadown bride who had her dearest wish – a white wedding? It snowed.

☆

Two Irishmen on a train. 'Oi wish we were goin' the other way,' said one.
'Why's that.'
''Cause oi like to sit with me back to the engine.'

☆

Patrick phoned the bank teller: 'This is a stick-up. Send me fifty thousand pounds.'

☆

A man started to tell his pal an Irish joke when he was interrupted.

'Look,' said the pal, 'I'm sick and tired of Irish jokes. Don't you know they're anti-racial?'

'Very well,' said the man, 'these two Chinamen were having a Guinness in a Belfast pub ...'

Kathleen signed the hotel register with an 'O'.

'Why don't you sign with an 'X'?' asked the clerk.

'Well, I used to sign it that way,' replied Kathleen, 'but when I got my divorce I took my maiden name.'

Unlucky? Brendan caught an incurable disease off a faith healer.

'Can you lend me your lawnmower?'

'Certainly ... just as long as you don't take it out of the garden.'

The Killarney hotel porter was told by the manager always to welcome guests by name. 'The name will be on the luggage,' he added.

Half an hour later, the porter was heard welcoming Mr and Mrs Simulated Leather.

'Does your wife cook by gas or electricity, Pat?'

'I dunno – I've never tried to cook her.'

An Irish Army officer was at a house of ill repute. 'Tell me,' he asked the madame, 'how much would you charge for my company?'

'Seeing you're in uniform,' came the reply, 'only five pounds.'

'That seems reasonable,' said the officer.

'*Company* – left, right, left, right ...'

☆

Michael: 'Well, my darling, we've won the pools – how about going on a world cruise?'

Mary: 'I'm not too keen. Couldn't we go somewhere else?'

☆

'Oi want a dog licence, please.'

'Certainly, sir – what name?'

'Rover.'

☆

Irish proverb: 'See a pin, pick it up, all day long you'll have a pin.'

☆

Did you hear about O'Brien's wallet transplant? He had to pay through the nose for it.

☆

Mind you, Finbarr's wife always stood by his side. She had to – they only had one chair.

☆

Then there was the Irish cannibal who became a vegetarian.

☆

At Murphy's funeral, one of the mourners remarked on the wonderful smile on his face.
'I know,' said his widow, 'it hasn't dawned on him yet.'

☆

Notice in a Co. Wicklow lane: 'When you can't see this sign, the river is under water.'

☆

'You'll have to go on a diet, Mrs O'Neil,' said the doctor. 'You can have four lettuce leaves, one piece of dry toast, a glass of orange juice and a tomato each day.'
'Very well, doctor. Do I take them before or after meals?'

☆

Outside a farm: 'Dog needed for milking cows.'

☆

Sean asked his landlady for a full-length mirror, explaining that he'd been out three times that week without his trousers.

☆

Did you hear about Murphy's whiskey diet? He's lost three days already.

☆

The exuberant father picked up his new baby son at the maternity hospital in Co. Kerry.
'I hope you're that baby's father,' said the ward nurse reprovingly.
'So do I, nurse, so do I,' came the reply.

☆

Muldoon was sounding off in the pub. 'All this talk about back seat drivers is rubbish,' he said. 'I've been driving for twenty-seven years, and I've never heard a word from behind.'
'What kind of car do you drive?'
'A hearse.'

Notice outside a social club in Cork: 'Closed tonight for official opening.'

Postman: 'I've a parcel here, but the name's obliterated.'
Mike: 'Can't be for me ... my name's O'Shaughnessy.'

Irish driver at garage: 'I'm in a hurry. Never mind the petrol – give me the stamps.'

'Are you a native of Cork?'
'Am I, hell, – I was born here.'

'Whenever you feel like a cigarette,' advised the doctor, 'put a carrot in your mouth.'
'I tried that, doctor,' said Sean, 'but it doesn't work.'
'Why not?'
'I can't get the carrot to stay alight.'

An old maid in a Ballycastle hotel complained to the manager: 'It's a disgrace, I tell you. I looked out of my window and saw a man taking a bath in a room across from mine.'

'But, madam,' said the manager, 'I can only see the top of the man's head.'

'Then just stand on this table ...'

☆

'My, that's a beautiful baby you have there, Mary.'

'Sure, that's nothing – you should see his photograph.'

☆

Magnus: 'How many feet in a yard?'

Patrick: 'It depends how many people are standing in it.'

☆

'How did the match go today, Michael?'

'Well ... we won the toss.'

☆

Murphy had a puncture, but his wife looked on the bright side. 'Sure, it's only the bottom that's flat,' she consoled him, 'the top's all right.'

☆

'I t'ink my mind's wandering, doctor.'

'Don't worry – it's too weak to go far.'

☆

How does an Irishman stop moles digging in his garden? He hides the spade.

☆

A guest in a Bray hotel was asked if he had slept well despite the crying of a baby in the next room. 'Of course I did,' he replied. 'When I take my teeth out, I can't hear a thing.'

☆

'Isn't the weather awful, Mrs O'Dowd?'
'It is an' all, but, sure, it's better than nothing.'

☆

Wife: 'I'm not saying I'm always right, Michael – I'm just saying you're always wrong.'

☆

Magnus: 'And your special subject is?'
Patrick: 'Brick laying.'

☆

What about the Irish goalkeeper who never stopped a ball? He thought that was what the net was for.

☆

A Cork man took a test to be a postman. The first question he was asked was: 'How far is the earth from the moon?'
He responded: 'If that's going to be my route – forget it.'

☆

On the menu of a Newry restaurant: Chicken in Harpic.

☆

41

Quite an achievement by the Waterford pot-holing club. They climbed Everest.

☆

For those who don't want to take part in our £5,000 crossword, the answers are on page 9. – *Irish paper*.

☆

Tourist: 'Any idea how many sheep are in this field?'
Mike: 'Sure – 386.'
'How on earth did you know that?'
'Easy … I counted the legs and divided by four.'

☆

They met on a blind date. He knew she was keen. She wore a wedding dress.

☆

Sign in a Cork shop: 'No smoking. Guide dogs excepted.'

☆

Irish hijacker: 'This is a cock-up.'
Pilot: 'Don't you mean a stick-up?'
'No – a cock-up. The gun's not loaded and I'm on the wrong plane.'

☆

Then there was the Killarney cowboy who wore paper trousers and was arrested for rustling.

☆

Magnus: 'What are pig skins for?'
Patrick: 'Holding pigs together.'

'Now, Mrs O'Connell, bend the knee, please.'
'Which way, doctor?'

☆

Ireland's first space satellite was launched, manned by astronaut Casey and a trained monkey. Over the Atlantic a signal lit up and the monkey made a few adjustments to the control.
Two hours later there was another signal and again the monkey carried out the manoeuvre.
Finally, Casey got impatient. 'When am I going to have something to do?' he asked ground control.
Two hours later came the signal: 'Control to Casey. Feed the monkey.'

☆

What about the Irish Uri Geller who stroked a spoon? His finger fell off.

☆

Experienced typist wants home typing. Reasonable rates. Sorry, no typewriter. – *Irish paper*.

☆

Did you hear about the Irishman who had jelly in one ear and custard in the other? He was a trifle deaf.

Irish Films are to make a sequel to *Raise the Titanic*: *Raise the Iceberg*.

☆

Magnus: 'Who invented the sword dance?'
Patrick: 'Someone who wanted to dance and cut his toenails at the same time.'

'What did the doctor say about you, Murphy?'
'He said I had acid indigestion.'
'Then you'd better stop drinking acid.'

☆

A Galway girl saw a sticker on the back of a car: 'If you can read this, you're too darn close.' She went along to a tailor, and asked to have the words embroidered on the knees of her tights.
'In script or italic?' asked the tailor.
'Neither,' came the reply, 'in Braille.'

☆

Ever been on an Irish package holiday? They pop you into a carton and send you air freight.

O'Grady lurched over the bar, spearing furiously at the olive in his glass. After it had eluded him half a dozen times, a man sitting next to him grabbed the toothpick and speared the olive first time.
'That's how you do it,' he boasted, handing over the olive.
'Big deal,' growled O'Grady. 'I already had him so tired he couldn't get away.'

☆

'Good morning, Mrs O'Mally, and how are you today?' asked the village postmistress.

'Very well thank you, Mrs Doyle. I've come to collect my pension.'

'Certainly. Do you have any means of identification?'

Sad about the Irish football team. The only win they had all season was when the pools panel picked them.

An old Galway farmer had to go into hospital for an operation. When he arrived, he was given a good bath.

As he left the bathroom, he said to the nurse: 'I'm glad *that's* over. I've been dreading that operation for years.'

Patrick bought a second-hand carpet, which he was assured was in mint condition. When he got it home, he found it had a hole in the middle.

Graffiti: KEEP IRELAND TIDY – STAY IN BED.

An Irish nuclear physicist went into a chemist's and asked: 'Could I have some prepared acetyl-salicyclic acid, please?'

'Do you mean aspirin?' asked the chemist.

'Yes, that's the stuff ... I can never remember it's name.'

A Cork driver was going round and round a city roundabout. A policeman stopped him and said: 'I've been watching you for an hour, and you've gone round that roundabout 247 times.'
'I know,' came the reply. 'It's not my fault, constable – my indicator's stuck.'

For sale, toilet seat cover, barely used. – *Irish paper*.

Post office clerk: 'You've addressed this parcel upside-down.'
'That's right,' said Mike, 'it's going to Australia.'

'I've just been to *Evita*, Mary.'
'Have you now? You don't look very brown.'

Sign in Wicklow shop: 'Haircuts half-price today. One per customer.'

Clancy and his mates went out for a meal. When they got the bill, Clancy checked it and asked: 'Which greedy swine ordered the Value Added Tax?'

Then there was the Cork man who bet on Beecher's Brook to win the Grand National.

The wife of a Dublin bank raider visited her husband in prison. Through the grill he whispered: 'Is the money still safely buried, Kathleen?'

'It couldn't be safer,' she assured him. 'They've gone and built a twenty-five-storey block of flats on top of it.'

☆

Car sticker in O'Connell Street, Dublin: BRUSH UP YOUR ERSE.

☆

How about the Gay Nineties party in Donegal? The men were all gay and the women were all ninety.

☆

'Come down, sir – you can't stand on top of this bus.'

'Why not?'

'It's a single-decker.'

☆

Seen on an Irish hospital notice board: 'Dangerous drugs must be locked up with the ward sister.'

☆

A man travelling home from a Dundalk race meeting, at which he'd lost all his money, passed the cemetery where one of his pals had been buried a few days before.

'Don't worry, Sean,' he called out. 'You're missin' nothin' here.'

☆

'What will I get Pat for his birthday, Mary?'
'How about a nice book?'
'No – he's got a book.'

☆

In Paris, when tables and chairs are out on the pavement, they call them cafés. In Ireland they call them evictions.

☆

How about the unsuccessful Irish burglar? His wife wouldn't let him out at night.

☆

'I've been taking the vitamin pills, doctor, but they don't seem to be doing me much good.'
'Perhaps it's your diet. What have you been eating?'
'Oh, are you supposed to eat too?'

☆

An Irishman invented a new deodorant called Invisible. You disappear and everyone wonders where the smell's coming from.

☆

Muldoon had bad luck with both his wives. The first one left him and the second one won't.

☆

'My new wellies are hurtin' me.'
'But you've got them on the wrong feet.'
'Sure, they're the only feet I have.'

☆

Paratrooper Mike was receiving instructions from the sergeant: 'After you jump, count to five and pull the first cord. If the 'chute doesn't open, pull the second cord to open the emergency parachute. After landing, you'll find a truck waiting to take you back to base.'

Mike made the jump, counted to five, and pulled the first cord. Nothing happened. He pulled the second cord and that faulted too.

'Typical,' said Mike. 'I bet there's no truck waiting for me down there, either.'

'For years we were perfectly happy, Bridget. He didn't drink, gamble or chase women.'

'Then what happened?'

'He came out of prison.'

Letter from a Killarney hotel-keeper: 'I should like to know, please, whether you want two bedrooms with double beds in them, or two double-bedded rooms, as I have only one double-bedded room; all the beds are double beds, except one in the double-bedded room, which is a single bed.'

'Wasn't it shockin' about that hotel disaster in Rome, Kathleen?'

'Indeed it was. There's nothin' worse than being killed on your holidays.'

As Mrs O'Sullivan observed to her husband at Stonehenge: 'You know, it hasn't really changed since we were here in 1978.'

☆

Sign in a Derry shop: 'Easy credit plan – one hundred per cent down and nothing to pay each month.'

'Why do you always have a packet of Daz on your telly?'
'I've no aerial.'

☆

Dublin Airport announcement: 'As a result of the strike by Aer Lingus staff, anyone wishing to fly to Glasgow will have to go by boat.'

☆

Irish boat-race cox: 'We're sinking – pass it on.'

☆

Tough luck on the Irish driver in the Brazil Grand Prix. He was leading all the way, then, having clocked up one hundred thousand miles, he stopped to change the oil.

☆

Magnus: 'Who was born in a stable and had thousands of followers?'
Patrick: 'Red Rum.'

☆

'As I've said before, Maureen, it's useless going to the Job Centre. They're only giving work to school-leavers. I'm thirty-seven years old.'
'Can't you tell them you were kept in?'

☆

As the Titanic was sinking, an Irishman rushed around shouting, 'Where's the dance? Where's the dance?'
Another passenger asked him, 'What do you mean "Where's the dance?" '
'Well,' came the reply, 'I keep hearing an announcement "*a-band-on ship, a-band-on ship*".'

☆

As Bridget said when she went to buy a bidet, 'It saves you having any blankets on the bed.'

☆

Shop sign in Galway: 'Fish and chips 60p, children 25p.'

☆

'First, the bad news,' said the doctor. 'We'll have to amputate both your legs.'
'And the good news?'
'There's a chap in the next ward who wants to buy your wellies.'

☆

Notice in a Kilkenny bar: 'Please do not leave while room is in motion.'

☆

A new Irish whodunnit has a surprise ending – the murderer is a character from another book.

A Cork man with one ear was standing at a bar.
'Would you like a drink?' asked a pal.
'No thanks,' he replied, 'I've one 'ere.'

☆

Irish pilot to passengers: 'Before we leave for Tenerife, we've got some crops to spray.'

☆

'Do you find it profitable to keep a cow, Michael?'
'Oh yes, my cow gives about eight quarts a day.'
'And how much of that do you sell?'
'Oh, about twelve quarts.'

☆

Then there was the jobless Irishman who went along to a Sale of Work.

☆

The artificial ski slope at Belfast has been closed because of snow and ice. – *News item.*

☆

Notice in an Irish hotel: 'Please do not lock the door, as we have lost the key.'

☆

Two brothers were meeting at Dublin Airport after a separation of forty-five years.
'Do you think you'll recognise him?' a friend asked one of the brothers.
'I don't suppose I will,' came the reply.
'And will he recognise you?'
'Without a doubt – sure, I haven't been away.'

☆

Magnus: 'What is the meaning of the word "Thistledown"?'
Patrick: 'Raining very hard.'

☆

Sean couldn't remember when his wife's birthday was, but he thought it was some time this year.

☆

Policeman: 'Anything you say may be held against you.'
Burglar: 'Miss Ireland.'

☆

In Ireland they sell Round About Eight Mints.

☆

A Kerry farmer came across a lorry stuck underneath a low bridge. He asked the driver, 'Tell me something ... where exactly are you takin' the bridge to?'

☆

The Irish TUC decided today that Wednesday's ballot will be secret. There'll be a show of hands but everyone will be blindfolded. – *News report.*

☆

A Killarney farmer dyed one of his lambs red and sold it for two hundred pounds. So he dyed all his lambs in bright colours ... and now he's the biggest lamb dyer in the Republic.

Definition of bravery: running in a men's relay race in a nudist camp.

☆

Barber: 'There … how do you like your hair?'
Neil: 'Quite nice, but a little longer at the back, please.'

☆

Spare a thought for the Irish boy whose mother bought his clothes from the Army and Navy Stores. He went to school as a Japanese admiral.

☆

And what about the Irish cat burglar who kept stealing cats?

☆

Trousers, excellent condition, worn once, 40″ waist. Three pairs £21, will split. – *Irish paper.*

☆

Then there was the Irishman who brought home a three-piece suite. 'How many times,' demanded his wife, 'have I told you *never* to accept suites from strangers?'

☆

Police in Dublin soon caught a persistent wool thief. They found he always worked to a pattern.

☆

Tourist Board warning on a cliff in the Republic: 'There is a drop of 500ft from this cliff. If you fall, the best view is to your left.'

☆

Notice in Wicklow newsagent: 'Wanted – steady young woman to wash, iron and milk two cows.'

☆

Then there was the Cork woman who wrote to all her friends saying she wouldn't be sending any Christmas cards because postage was so dear.

☆

'Did you stamp the crate "THIS SIDE UP WITH CARE"?' asked the curator.
'Indeed I did,' came the reply, 'and, just to make sure, I put it on the bottom as well.'

☆

'Would you like to buy a pocket calculator, Mike?'
'No thanks – I know how many pockets I have.'

☆

The priest rang the Health Board to report a dead donkey outside his house.
'But I thought *you* looked after the dead,' quipped the clerk.
'We do,' agreed the priest, 'but only after we have contacted the relatives.'

Pat and Mick went into orbit in the first Irish space rocket.
Pat went on a space walk, and, returning to the rocket knocked on the capsule door.
'Who's there?' asked Mick.

☆

'What do you mean – *sacked*, Sean? I thought you were a Tube train driver for life.'
'So did I – but they caught me overtaking.'

A factory to make a new type of video recorder has opened in the Republic. It tapes all the programmes you hate, then plays them back while you're on holiday.

☆

In an Irish school party to a big game at Wembley the teacher gave out the tickets with the pupils' names written on the back.
One pupil, who was waving his ticket around, was warned: 'Don't do that — if anyone snatches it, they'll be in the ground instead of you.'
'No, he won't,' replied the boy. 'It's got my name on it.'

☆

Factory inspector: 'This machine should have a warning on it not to go too near.'
Foreman Pat: 'Yes, I know. We did have one, but no one ever got hurt, so we took it down.'

☆

Notice to staff in a Bangor hotel: 'All fire extinguishers must be examined at least 10 days before every fire.'

☆

'I'm finished with gambling, Sean.'
'I don't believe it.'
'I'll bet you a fiver.'

☆

Magnus: 'What's the difference between a cow and a bull?'
Patrick: 'A cow gives you milk and a bull gives you Bovril.'

Advert in an Irish paper: 'Before using your hair tonic, I had three bald patches. Now I have only one.'

☆

Did you hear about the Irishman who played truant from the Open University? He sent back empty envelopes.

☆

The doctor told Mary to take the medicine one day, skip the next, take it the next day, skip the next, and so on.
A fortnight later, Mary came back and said she felt no better.
'Did you take the medicine as instructed?' asked the doctor.
'Indeed I did,' replied Mary, 'but all that skipping fairly took it out of me.'

☆

Irish proverb: Show me a man that smiles at defeat, and I'll show you a happy chiropodist.

☆

On a Galway menu: Cook's Special – Shiska Bog.

☆

'I'm looking for a romantic birthday card, Miss.'
'How about this one – *To the only girl I ever loved?*'
'That's great – I'll take four.'

A population survey in the Republic today shows that priests have the lowest divorce rate. – *News item*.

Then there was the Irishman who bought a wrist watch on tick.

Murphy broke his leg and the doctor put it in a cast. 'On no account climb stairs till the cast has been removed,' the doctor warned him.
Six weeks later an X-ray showed the leg had mended. 'Can I climb stairs now?' asked Murphy.
'Certainly,' replied the doctor.
'Thank heaven for that – I'm sick and tired of shinning up the drainpipe.'

Magnus: 'Who was the first woman on earth?'
Patrick: 'Give me a clue.'
Magnus: 'Think of an apple.'
Patrick: 'Granny Smith.'

Sign on a road in Co. Wicklow: 'Last garage till the next one.'

'Could I have a big bunch of flowers, please? My wife's just had triplets.'
'Yes of course ... would you like a vase to put them in?'
'No thanks, we've got a pram.'

Why are there no Irish astronauts? They have to pay their own expenses.

'Hey, Michael, is the water in the pool hot?'
'It's freezing but it soon warms up.'
'In that case I'll wait another fifteen minutes for it to get really warm.'

The holiday representative in Spain showed the Derry man where he could buy his water in bottles.
'Thanks very much,' he said. 'How many will I need to have a bath?'

What do Irish geologists keep their rocks in? Rock sacks.

Then there was the Irishman who took pot to improve his snooker.

'Do you sell kid gloves?'
'We do indeed. What size kid?'

What about the Irish Dalek that went steady with a dustbin?

☆

Mike in restaurant: 'About my soup.'
'Yes, sir?'
'The fly in it was cold.'

☆

Then there was the Limerick man who used an electric blanket on his water bed and woke up poached.

☆

Kelly didn't do much better. He went to a stag party and found his wife was the star.

☆

Not forgetting the blind Irishman who went on a deaf date.

☆

And what about the pub in Letterkenny that hired a famous entertainer to knock down a pile of drunks?

☆

Thieves stole all the toilets from a Lurgan police station. Police don't have a thing to go on. – *News item*.

☆

'Why do you call your newt Tiny, Sean?'
'Because he's my-newt.'

☆

Pat: 'Are you goin' to a party with that crate of Guinness?'
Mike: 'No – I'm movin' house.'

☆

Did you hear about the Irishman whose standard of living rocketed after he acquired a credit card? He found he could open front doors with it.

☆

Irish snooker commentator: 'He's chanced his arm and it's come off.'

☆

When Columbus arrived in America he found a note saying: 'I was here first. Bad Luck. St Brendan the Navigator.'

☆

Then there was the Dublin man who invented a waterproof teabag.

☆

Lawyer: 'I wish I could have done more for you.'
O'Malley: 'Don't worry – fifteen years is plenty.'

☆

Top of the charts on Irish TV is the best of the weather forecasts repeats.

☆

What about the Irish prison warder who put a crowd of unruly prisoners in solitary together?

61

Sentry: 'Halt! Who goes there?'
Irish recruit: 'Nobody – it's me comin' back.'

☆

'Would you like to try our new oatmeal soap, madam?'
'No thanks – I never wash my oatmeal.'

☆

Sardines must be Irish. Who else would lock themselves in a tin and leave the key on the outside?

☆

Notice in a Cork chemist: 'We dispense with accuracy.'

☆

Sad about the Irish mosquito. It died of malaria.

☆

'Did you enjoy *Chariots of Fire*, Brendan?'
'Not as much as *Ben-Hur*.'

☆

It could only happen to an Irish actor. He failed the audition for *Crossroads*.

☆

Magnus: 'Which month has twenty-eight days?'
Pat: 'All of them.'

☆

Early to bed and early to rise means you never see anyone else. – *Irish proverb*.

☆

'Isn't it amazing,' remarked Tim, 'that just enough things happen every day to fill your newspaper?'

Irish Goldilocks: Who's been sleeping in my porridge?'

TV reporter to an Irish fan at Liverpool-Everton Milk Cup Final: 'What do you think the final score will be?'
'Three each.'
'Three each?'
'Yes – three for Rush, three for Souness and three for Dalglish.'

'Sorry, sir, we don't sell two-by-three size wood any more. It's 5.1 centimetres by 7.65 centimetres.'
'How much is it now then?'
'20p a foot.'

Notice in Dublin supermarket: 'Wanted, price tag changer. Must be fast worker.'

'Want to buy your wife a leopard skin coat for a fiver, Dennis?'
'What's it like?'
'Absolutely spotless.'

Then there was the Irishman who donated his organs to Belfast Cathedral and the Tower Ballroom, Blackpool.

Irish small ad: Passport for sale. Owner going abroad.

☆

Then there was the Irish jury foreman who was found not guilty.

☆

A Kerry girl was stopped in the street by a reporter and asked what she thought of Red China.
'It's all right,' she replied, 'as long as it doesn't clash with the tablecloth.'

☆

A man in a pub at Howth boasted he could drink 20 pints at one go. Another bet him a fiver he couldn't. The man left the bar, came back, and drank twenty pints one after the other.
'Why did you leave the bar?' asked the loser, handing over the fiver.
'Well,' came the reply, 'I just went into the pub across the road to see if I could do it.'

☆

A pity about the Irish down-and-out who became addicted to Harpic. He went clean round the bend.

☆

What about the Irishman who took his missus to a wife-swapping party? He got a kettle.

☆

'Is it true, Michael, that the Clancy Brothers are really brothers?'
'Sure it is. And so are the Nolan Sisters.'

☆

Pat and Mike were planning to rob a bank. 'I'll stay in the car and take all the risks,' said Pat.
'Risks?'
'Yes – the car's not taxed.'

☆

You can soon tell if you're at an Irish soccer match. The programme carries the lyrics of *Why Are We Waiting*.

☆

Sad about the Irish fell-walker. He broke a leg.

☆

Car sticker: 'No hand signals – driver from Ireland.'

☆

How about the Irish barman who was on the receiving end of a £50 forged note? He insisted on the customer paying with two £25 coins.

☆

Notice in a Cork doctor's waiting-room: 'Please have all your symptoms ready.'

☆

Irish receptionist: 'I'm afraid the chairman is out, but if it's really important he'll see you.'

☆

Shop sign in Waterford: 'Bargain basement, first floor.'

☆

'I hear Sean was in hospital. How is he?'
'Not too good, Bridget. They gave him a post mortem yesterday.'

☆

As Maureen explained in the Missing Persons Bureau: 'It's not that I want my husband back – but I'd like to know what he's up to.'

☆

Then there was the Irish nail biter who gave himself up for Lent.

☆

'Did you hear that Seamus drowned?'
'Glory be – what happened?'
'Seems he took acupuncture treatment on a water bed.'

☆

Irish clairvoyant killed in coach crash. – *Irish Times*.

☆

Dublin bingo caller: 'Sherwood Forest – all the trees, thirty-tree.'

☆

'Why do you only drink heavy beer, Molloy?'
'So the police won't lift me.'

☆

Trust an Irish doctor to discover a completely new cure for which there is no known disease.

☆

A set of traffic lights were stolen from a junction at Cork. A police spokesman said, 'Some thieves will stop at nothing.' – *Cork Examiner*.

☆

Shop sign: 'Free estimates at almost no cost.'

☆

'About those birds and bees you were telling me about, Mum.'
'Yes. Michael?'
'Why don't they take the pill?'

☆

Rings can be ordered by post. Simply state size required, or enclose string tied around your finger. – *Irish paper*.

☆

'I hear your wife's got a microwave oven, Sean?'
'That's right – now she can ruin a meal in half the time.'

☆

Notice in a Galway butcher: 'Try our pre-war sausages.'

☆

Spare a thought for the Irishman who lost his luggage on holiday. The cork came out the bottle.

☆

Irish patient to fellow in next bed: 'Look, the doctor's coming round soon. Try to cheer him up because he's very worried about you.'

☆

Did you hear about the Irish Moss Bros? At the first stroke of midnight the trousers fall down.

☆

Irish graffiti: 'You can always count on your fingers.'

☆

For sale, beautiful wedding dress. Only worn twice. – *Irish paper*.

☆

'Why do you put three cherries and a sliced banana in your beer, Sean?'
'The doctor told me to eat more fruit.'

☆

Sign in Tipperary shop: 'Special Offer. Ears pierced while you wait. Pay for two and get another ear pierced free.'

☆

Then there was the Irish burglar who was found not guilty and said he would appeal.

☆

What about the Irish model who was hired to model for *Playboy*? She asked if she had to bring her own staples.

☆

Just Mike's luck. He backed the winner of the Grand National each way – but it only went one way.

☆

Why did the Irishman cross a dog with a jeep?
He wanted a Land Rover.

☆

Road sign: LAST GUINNESS FOR 30 MILES.

☆

They've started a Dole Protection Society in
Dublin. You pay ten pence a week, and if the dole
people find you a job, the DPS fights your case.

☆

'Didn't your wife mind you staying out all
weekend, Mick?'
'Not a bit of it. I was going to have my front teeth
out anyway.'

☆

Then there was the Irish tailor who took a
customer's inside waist measurement.

☆

Shop sign: 'Don't get overcharged in other shops –
come in here!'

☆

What about the Cork man who took out blanket
insurance because he smokes in bed?

☆

'Why didn't you stay for the second act of the play,
Sean?'
'Sure, it said in the programme: "Act two, three
weeks later." '

☆

'Are Vasectomies Hereditary?' – headline in *Irish paper*.

'Mum, can we watch the solar eclipse?'
'All right – but mind you don't get too close.'

Magnus: 'What does "unaware" mean?'
Patrick: 'The last thing you take off at night.'

'How are you getting on with that medicine I prescribed for you, Leary?'
'I haven't started it yet, doctor.'
'Why on earth not?'
'The label says to keep the cap screwed tightly on the bottle.'

Two Irishmen were planning what to wear at a fancy dress ball.
'It's just a pity there aren't three of us,' said one.
'Why's that?'
'We could have gone as Alias Smith and Jones.'

Shop sign: 'Closing down. Thanks to all our customers.'

Did you hear about the Irish con man who was released from jail recently? He had five more years to serve.

Then there was the Dublin man at the Mint who threatened to strike unless he made less money.

☆

Policeman: 'Are you the owner of this car, sir?'
Michael: 'Actually, it's an automatic — but I've got to be with it.'

☆

How about the Belfast man who got the VC? They cured him.

☆

On a church notice board: 'Daily services. Come early if you want a back seat.'

☆

Magnus: 'What's the letter "L" stand for on a car?'
Patrick: 'Learner.'
Magnus: 'And what does "GB" mean?'
Patrick: 'Getting Better.'

☆

Did you hear about the Irish Quasimodo? He bought an off-the-peg suit in O'Connell Street.

☆

A woman went into a baker's in Tipperary, and asked for some hot cross buns but was given plain ones.
When she complained, the girl retorted, 'These *are* hot cross buns, but without the cross.'

☆

How can you spot an Irish optician's eye chart? The spelling has been corrected.

☆

'Are those two dogs Jack Russells, Muldoon?'
'No – one's mine and the other's my brother's.'

☆

What about the Newry man who declined an invitation to join a fife band? He explained he didn't like bananas.

☆

Spare a thought for the Irish sportsman on crutches. He jumped over the net at table tennis.

☆

Theatre poster: 'Book early to be sure of disappointment.'

☆

Then there was the Irish SAS squad which stormed Dublin Zoo and freed all the ostriches.

☆

'I think I'm changing sex, doctor.'
'Why's that?'
'I keep getting letters addressed "Dear Sir or Madam".'

☆

Dear Sirs,

When I buy your biscuits, I notice that the top biscuit in the packet is nearly always broken. So may I suggest that in future you leave out the top biscuit in each packet?

☆

Notice in a pub in Eire: 'This establishment closes at 11 pm sharp. We are open from 9.30 am. If you haven't had enough to drink in that time the management feels you haven't really been trying.'

☆

Car sticker: VAL DOONICAN IS OFF HIS ROCKER

☆

What do you call an Irishman who's been dead for fifty years?
Peat.

☆

Magnus: 'What are nitrates?'
Patrick: 'Cheaper than day rates.'

☆

Then there was the fan who stopped following Sligo Rovers because he said it was a waste of toilet rolls.

☆

What is an Irishman's favourite TV show?
Plankety-Plank.

☆

Librarian: 'Are you looking for light reading or something heavy, sir?'
'It doesn't matter – I've got the car outside.'

Did you hear about the Irish egg-timer that's an hour fast?

Irish definition of heredity: If your Mum and Dad can't have kids, neither can you.

Trust an Irishman to invent a silencer for a back-seat driver.

Burial and cremation charges in Ireland are going up fifty-five per cent to keep pace with the cost of living. – *News item.*

Irish farmer in London hotel: 'What are the meal times?'
Receptionist: 'Breakfast from seven to eleven, lunch from twelve to three, tea from four-thirty to six, and dinner from seven to ten-thirty.'
'Glory be ... when am I going to see the town?'

An Irishman at work on the roof of a fifteen-storey building suddenly dived over with outstretched arms.

'What did you do that for, my son?' asked the priest.

'Well,' came the reply, 'I just got a bit tired of hearing my foreman bragging about how he used to fly Wellingtons during the war.'

☆

Did you hear about the Irish Avon lady? She goes from house to house buying cosmetics.

☆

'Can I have a Mother's Day card, please?'
'Certainly – who's it for?'

☆

Trust an Irishman to dream up Anglers Anonymous. You dial a number and listen to a pack of lies.

☆

Paddy to driving instructor: 'Can I drive in my wellies?'
Instructor: 'Let's start with the car first.'

☆

What about the Irishman who asked in the Tate Gallery for a two pound bag of sugar?

☆

Sean went to see a psychiatrist. The psychiatrist drew a circle on a piece of paper and asked, 'What does this remind you of?'

'A naked woman,' replied Sean.

The psychiatrist drew a square. 'How about this?' he asked.

'A naked woman out for a walk.'

Then the psychiatrist drew a triangle.

Said Sean: 'A naked woman sitting down.'

'Well, well,' remarked the psychiatrist, 'you're certainly preoccupied with sex, aren't you?'

'What do you mean?' asked Sean. 'It's you who's drawing all the naughty pictures.'

How about the Irish learner driver who stopped ... and stopped ... at a crossroads controlled by a policeman.

'Why aren't you going ahead?' asked the instructor.

'Well, you see,' came the reply, 'I'm waiting for him to turn green.'

Sign in a gift shop in Killarney: 'No credit given — except to people over eighty-five accompanied by both parents.'

Air hostess: 'We are now approaching Aldergrove Airport, Belfast. Please put your watches back two hundred years.'

'I think my wife will live forever, Brendan.'
'How do you make that out?'
'She says she's nothing to wear except dresses she wouldn't be seen dead in.'

Never tell an Irishman a joke with a double meaning. He won't get either of them.

Then there was the Cork dog breeder who went broke and had to call in the official retriever.

A Limerick caller had difficulty dialling Australia so he asked the operator to try the number.
'Do you have the area code?' she asked.
'No,' came the reply, 'it's just a bug that's going around.'

An advert for a forty-eight-hour film print service in a Post Office magazine in the Republic included this cautionary advice: 'Please allow for postal delays.'

Did you hear about the man who went to a boxing match in Belfast? A football match broke out.

Dolphins are so intelligent that within weeks of captivity they can train an Irishman to stand on the edge of their pool and throw them fish three times a day.

A Kerry man went to a Chinese takeaway the other night – and took away two Chinese.

☆

You can always tell when you're in a restaurant with an Irishman. The waiter brings a menu without joined up writing.

☆

'Do you sell monogrammed hankies?'
'Yes we do, sir. Which initial would you like?'
'What have you got?'

☆

Then there was the Cork man who got the sack from a massage parlour for rubbing people up the wrong way.

☆

Bingo-calling priest: 'All the Disciples, number twelve … Three Wise Men, number three … All the Commandments, number ten …'

☆

Sign in a Galway barber's shop: 'During alterations, customers will be shaved in the rear.'

☆

'Are these pills habit-forming, doctor?'
'No, Mrs O'Mally, not as long as you take them regularly.'

☆

Ulstermen are the most perfectly balanced people in the world: they've got a chip on both shoulders.

☆

Patrick always was unlucky. He even won the football pools the same week as his boss.

☆

During a bank strike in the Republic, a customer phoned to ask if the bank was functioning.
'Yes,' replied the manager, 'we have two windows open.'
'Does that mean,' asked the customer, 'I can't come in through the front door?'

☆

Car sticker: IRISH YOUNG FARMERS DO IT IN WELLIES.

☆

What about the Tipperary man who went looking for streetwalkers in Venice?

☆

Only an Irish author could come up with *The ABD of Snooker*.

☆

Spare a thought for the Kerry man who won a tea trolley in a raffle. He only drinks coffee.

☆

'Oi've just seen some cows crossin' the road.'
'Was someone drivin' them?'
'No – they were walkin'.'

☆

While researching a feature about life in a Belfast prison, a reporter asked an inmate: 'Do you watch much television here?'

'Only in the daytime,' came the reply. 'At night, we're locked in our cells.'

'Oh, well,' said the reporter, 'it's nice that you're allowed to watch during the day at least.'

'*Nice?*' asked the prisoner. 'Sure, that's part of the punishment!'

Then there was the Waterford woman with a severe case of marital thrombosis. She was married to a clot.

'Do you call this a ploughman's lunch?'

'Well, dat's all a ploughman gets if he has his lunch here.'

Scientists crossed an Irishman with a homing pigeon and got a parrot that keeps landing and asking the way.

Sign on an Irish building site: 'Night watchman patrols this area twenty-four hours a day.'

What about the Antrim man who was buried in a pauper's grave? The pauper objected.

A Kerry mother named her baby son after the entire local shinty team. She wasn't sure which of them was the father.

☆

Translation on an Irish menu: 'Coq au vin ... chicken in a lorry.'

☆

A TV salesman demonstrated the latest colour set to a Cork housewife. To show how powerful the remote control device was, he operated it from the bathroom.
A few days later a neighbour asked her how she liked her new colour TV.
'The picture's lovely,' she replied, 'but it's a bit of a nuisance having to go to the bathroom every time you want to change channels.'

☆

Four hippies at an Irish pop festival were taken to hospital with head injuries after drinking milk. The cow sat down.

☆

What about the Irish scientist who dreamed up the idea of breeding sardines the exact size to fit the tin?

☆

Not forgetting the Irish snooker player who sank three lagers and a double gin.

☆

81

Kevin went to the dentist to have all his teeth out. When he came out he remarked to his friend, 'Never again.'

Muldoon is half-Irish and half-Scottish. Half of him wants to get drunk while the other half doesn't want to pay for it.

'My husband never makes a mess when he paints, Mary. He uses the paint that doesn't drip.'
'You're lucky, Beatrice. I've got the drip that doesn't paint.'

A Howth man was filling in an application for credit. Among the questions was, 'Length of residence in present location?'
After some thought, he wrote: '65 feet, including outside toilet.'

Five hundred cases of Kit-E-Kat were stolen from a warehouse in Dublin last night. Police are looking for a cat with a heavy goods vehicle licence. – *News Item*.

Sign in a watch repairer's in Kilkenny: 'Having a short holiday to unwind.'

An Irish couple at Windsor Castle were trying to make themselves heard above the roar of low-flying jet aircraft.

'It's a wonder,' said the wife, 'they built it so close to Heathrow Airport.'

'Murphy, are you going to eat this dinner, or will I give it to the dog?'
'Why, what did the dog do?'

Irish weather forecast: 'Partly cloudy, somewhat cooler with local showers, followed by a hurricane.'

Seamus was driving down the middle of the road at a hundred miles per hour when he was stopped by the police. 'I'm allowed to,' he pleaded with them. 'It says on my licence: "Tear along the dotted line."'

I wouldn't say the flight from Belfast to Dublin was slow, but the in-flight movie was *Gone With The Wind*.

Irish clairvoyant: 'I charge £12 for two questions.'
'Isn't that rather high?'
'Yes – what's your second question?'

Notice in a Galway police station: 'Will the person who took the cake from the duty sergeant's desk kindly return same. It is needed as evidence in a food poisoning case.'

☆

Magnus: 'Who won the Boat Race in 1982?'
Patrick: 'Can I have two guesses?'

☆

An Irishman received a ticket for *Live From Her Majesty's*. He turned up to see the show at Buckingham Palace.

☆

Sign on a country road in Co. Wicklow: 'Detour – drive sideways.'

☆

'Is it true Beatrice is in *Who's Who*?'
'No – she's in *What's That*?'

☆

Irish restaurant sign: 'Customers who pay for their meal and leave without eating will be prosecuted.'

☆

Sean stood in the dock, charged with drunken driving. 'The last time you were here,' said the judge, 'I told you I didn't want to see you again.'
'That's what I told the policeman, your honour, but he breathalysed me anyway.'

An Irishman bought a packet of self-addressed envelopes, but later returned them to the shop and complained that they didn't.

☆

'Good evening, sir. Do you have a TV licence?'
'Of course I have – I bought one when they first came out in 1946.'

☆

An Irishman called at the local police station and asked to see the man who had robbed his home the previous night.
He wanted to know how the thief managed to get in without waking up his wife.

☆

Two Irish counterfeiters went into the countryside to try and unload some £18 notes.
In the first shop they found, they asked the shopkeeper if he would change the note.
'No problem,' he replied. 'Would two sevens and a four be all right?'

☆

A bad sport, Bridget. When her toddler didn't win the Baby Show, she demanded a saliva test.

☆

An Irishman went to the doctor to find out what made him tick ... and chime the hours and quarters.

☆

Sign on an Irish spiritualist's door: 'Please ring – knocking causes confusion.'

☆

Priest: 'Did you ever sleep with a woman?'
'Well, Father, I might have dozed off once or twice.'

☆

'Doctor, I'm suffering from hallucinations.'
'Nonsense, O'Reilly, you're imagining things.'

☆

A Cork man complained to the Tourist Board about his Blackpool hotel: 'For dinner we had two potatoes. One of them was bad and the other one was an onion.'

☆

Derry chemist: 'If this medicine doesn't work, come back and I'll have another go at making out the doctor's handwriting.'

☆

Sticker seen in Liverpool: IMPORTED IRISH CAR – BACK-SEAT DRIVE.

☆

A campaign has been launched in the Republic for people to donate their kidneys for heart transplants.

☆

Then there was the Irishman being sworn in at court – who held the card in his left hand and read out the Bible.

☆

Not forgetting the Irish docker who said he'd never had a day's illness in his life. He always made it last a week.

☆

'Did Patrick say anything before he passed on?'
'Yes – "How can they sell it for 65p a bottle?" '

☆

Sign in a Belfast crematorium car park: 'Positively no exit from here.'

☆

Sean always drives with the emergency brake on. Then if an emergency happens he's ready for it.

☆

Sign on the bottom of a toilet door in Piccadilly: 'Beware of Irish limbo dancers.'

Two Irishmen finished their drinks in a country pub and drove to Dublin.
After a while, one said: 'We're getting closer to town.'
'What makes you think so?'
'We're hittin' more people.'

Brendan refused to buy an electric toothbrush. He didn't know whether his teeth were AC or DC.

☆

And what about Michael, who thought his wife had stopped smoking cigarettes because he found cigar butts around the house.

☆

What did the Irishman say to the chiropodist?
Me fate is in your hands.

☆

Did you hear about the Kerry man who received a new phone book? He added his name after the last entry and sent copies to the first six names on the list.

☆

'I don't know what to give the wife for our silver wedding.'
'Why don't you just ask her?'
'I don't want to spend that much.'

☆

Did you hear about the new Irish Express card?
It's like an American Express card, only no one accepts it.

☆

'I wish we didn't have to put the clocks forward every year, Michael.'
'Why's that?'
'Mine keeps falling off the mantelpiece.'

☆

The judge heard the charges, and then asked, 'Are you the defendant in this case?'

'No, your honour,' came the reply. 'I've a lawyer to do the defending. I'm the chap who done it.'

The good news is that coal has been discovered in the Irish Sea. The bad news is that it's too wet to burn.

Then there was the Irishman who had ambitions to be a sex maniac, but he failed his practical.

Sign on the door of an Irish café: 'Sorry, we're open.'

A girl approached a man in a Cork street and asked him to buy a raffle ticket for a turkey.

'I'm sorry,' came the reply, 'I can't eat turkey. It doesn't agree with me.'

'Never mind,' said the girl. 'You aren't likely to win it anyway.'

'In that case,' said the man, 'I'll take six tickets.'

What about the Irish couple who named their test tube baby Pyrex?

Irish hospital poster: PLEASE HELP OUR NUR-SES HOME.

Then there was the Ballykelly clairvoyant who was granted a divorce on the grounds of her husband's adultery in Limerick the next weekend.

Killarney landlady to guests: 'We don't get up early on Sundays, so just lie in bed till you hear me scraping the toast.'

When a census taker called at a cottage in an Irish village, he was told: 'We don't want any. We're not buyin' nothin'.'
'But I'm not selling anything,' said the census man. 'I'm here to find out how many people there are in Ireland.'
'Well, you're wastin' your time,' came the reply. 'I haven't the faintest idea.'

Did you hear about the Cork woman who was married so often she had a drip-dry wedding dress?

An Irish football team signed a Jewish inside-right, but later sacked him because he wouldn't part with the ball.

'Look, Bridget, it says here that it takes seven Angora goats to make one of those fluffy-looking sweaters.'

'My ... isn't it wonderful what they can teach animals to do nowadays?'

Patrick finished his five-course meal and called over the waiter.

'I'd like a double brandy and detergent,' he said.

'Why detergent?' asked the waiter.

'To wash up,' came the reply. 'I've no money to pay the bill.'

Graffiti: 'I'M GAY AND IRISH – I GO OUT WITH GIRLS.'

A Dublin man has invented a revolutionary new fire alarm. It's made of unbreakable glass.

Two Belfast men were sweltering in a heatwave on a Spanish beach on 12 July.

Says one: 'I've just remembered the date – it's the twelfth.'

'So it is,' said the other. 'Aren't they gettin' a great day for it?'

An Irish scientist has invented a pill that's guaranteed to get rid of acne, oily skin and dandruff. After three months your head falls off.

'Can I tap you for a fiver, Sean?'
'For a fiver you can hit me with a brick.'

☆

Graffiti: THE WELSH ARE IRISHMEN WHO
LEARNT TO SWIM.

☆

Personnel officer: 'How many A levels do you
have?'
Mike: 'Seventy-three.'
'Seventy-three? You must be joking.'
'Well, you started it.'

☆

Sign in a Belfast shop: Sale of wellies, left foot
only.

☆

Did you hear about the Irish foam mattress? It's a
waterbed with Guinness.

☆

A doctor in Galway was called out at 4 am to make
a house call. Reluctantly, he got dressed and braved
a snowstorm. After examining the patient, he
advised him to send for a priest, relatives, friends,
and to make a will.
When the doctor got home and told his wife what
he had done, she asked, 'Was he really that bad?'
'Oh, no,' replied the doctor, 'but I wasn't going to
be the only sucker called out on a night like this.'

Then there was the Irish human cannonball – who had to get loaded first.

'Do you want a room with a bath or a shower?' asked the Irish hotel clerk.
'What's the difference?' asked the guest.
'Well, if you want a bath you sit down.'

How about the man who caused a bit of a flap at Dublin Zoo? He fed the penguins. To the lions.

A restaurant in Galway has Chicken à la Nolan on the menu. It doesn't taste very nice but everyone gets a leg.

Two Irishmen were out shooting duck. The first took aim, fired, and a duck landed at his feet.
'You could have saved that shot,' said his mate. 'The fall would have killed it anyway.'

'I'd like to apply for the job of temporary gravedigger.'
'Very well ... but we just want someone to fill in.'

Then there was the Kerry couple who got married in bathtubs because they wanted a double-ring ceremony.

Irish soccer fan: 'We've got a great team this year. No losses, no draws, and no goals scored against us.'
'How many games have you played?'
'The first is next Saturday.'

Pat thought his bank was in trouble. He had a ten pound cheque returned marked 'No funds'.

Sad about the Irishman at the Olympics who jumped the high hurdles instead of the low hurdles and shattered his personal best.

Then there was the Cork man who won't buy a fall-out shelter. He'll wait and buy a used one later.

'This non-stop rain reminds me of the Great Flood, Mike.'
'The *what*?'
'The Great Flood ... you know, Noah and the Ark.'
'Sure, I wouldn't know about that. I haven't had the telly on all week.'

Patrick's wife decided she would leave her drunken husband, but a neighbour persuaded her to give him one last chance.

'Instead of nagging him,' she advised, 'treat him nicely. Then he'll feel so ashamed he'll stop drinking.'

So the next night, when Patrick staggered home, his wife made him a cup of tea, warmed his slippers, loosened his collar and tie, and stroked his head.

'Shall we go to bed?' she suggested coyly.

'Might as well,' replied Patrick. 'If I go home now there'll only be a row.'

Sean wrote to the Ombudsman to complain he only got a five-minute break at the factory, while his mates enjoyed fifteen minutes.

The Ombudsman visited the factory and found it was true. 'Why are you discriminating against Sean?' he asked the manager.

'Well,' came the reply, 'it's like this. If I give him more than five minutes we'll have to retrain him.'

Then there was the Larne man who asked for a get-well card in German. His girl friend had measles.

'I seem to recall you were up before me three years ago,' said the judge, 'also for stealing a coat?'

'True, your honour. But how long do you think coats last?'

Hold-up man: 'Hand over everything in the till.'
Irish cobbler: 'Ready Friday.'

Did you hear about the Kerry man who put a silencer on his shotgun because his daughter wanted a quiet wedding?

'It's impossible for my wife to be pregnant, doctor. I've been at sea for over a year.'
'I know,' explained the doctor, 'but it's what we in the medical profession called a "grudge pregnancy".'
'What exactly's that?'
'In layman's terms ... someone had it in for you.'

The Irish jury's decision was unanimous ... that they send out for another barrel of Guinness.

A Cork man applying for a job was told the firm was overstaffed.
'Sure, but you could still hire me,' he pleaded. 'The little bit of work that I'd do would never be noticed.'

☆

Why are Irish wellies stamped TIF?
Toes In First.

☆

'What's the height requirement for the police, Tim?'
'Five foot eight inches.'
'Damn – I'm an inch too tall.'

Magnus: 'Who was Joan of Arc?'
Patrick: 'Noah's wife.'

'Thirty-five pounds to paint my garage? I wouldn't pay Michelangelo that much!'
'Listen – if he does the job for any less we'll come and picket you!'

One thing about Mary – she never repeats gossip. If you don't hear it first time, you've missed it.

An Irish driver tried to talk a traffic warden out of giving him a ticket. 'What do you do,' he asked, 'when you find someone who is *really* guilty?'
'I couldn't say,' replied the warden. 'All I ever book are the innocent ones.'

Pity about the Irish Test match that had to be abandoned. Both sides showed up wearing white.

'If you don't stop publishing Irish Jokes,' a man wrote to *Dublin Opinion*, 'I'll stop borrowing your magazine.'

97

'I'm sure our three kids are going to be doctors.'
'How do you make that out?'
'Sure, they never come when you call them!'

Kelly was worried about his young son, so he took him to a psychologist.
'Tell me, son,' asked the psychologist, 'how many wheels does a car have?'
'Four,' answered the boy.
'Now ... what is it that a cow has four of that a woman has two of?'
'Legs.'
'What does your father have that your mother likes most?'
'Money.'
The psychologist turned to Kelly and said: 'Your boy is fine ... there's nothing to worry about.'
'Thank heaven for that,' said Kelly, 'I got the last two questions wrong myself.'

Policeman: 'Can you describe your missing cashier, Mr Muldoon?'
'Well, now ... he's about 5 ft 8 in tall and £25,000 short.'

Sign in an Irish village shop: 'Please test matches before leaving shop.'

'Are you sure this cowhide jacket is good material, Mr O'Shaughnessy?'
'Of course it is. It held the cow together, didn't it?'

They've a smashing soccer team at Mountjoy Prison, Dublin. The only trouble is the governor won't let them play away from home.

☆

Customer collecting coat from cleaner's: 'Just a minute, there's a big stain on the sleeve.'
Assistant: 'You can't blame us for that. It was there when you brought it in.'

☆

Pat: 'Why is it I have 17 kids and you have none?'
John: 'I use the safe period.'
Pat: 'When's that?'
John: 'When you're on the night shift.'

☆

Note on a box of fish posted by a firm in the Irish Republic: 'If not delivered in 10 days, never mind.'

☆

Typist to manager: 'I've had all the criticism of my work I can take. How do you spell "quit"?'

☆

After a long run of defeats, Sligo Rovers tried a new training technique. Eleven dustbins were set out on the field and the players were told to imagine these were the opposition and dribble round them. The dustbins won 5-1.

☆

Did you hear about the two Irishmen who were sent to paint the porch of a TV celebrity? On his return, he found his £25,000 silver Porche had been treated to a coat of cream gloss.

Trust an Irishman to write to the papers to ask why there's only one Monopoly Commission.

A man took his dog into the pub. When the football scores came on TV and it was announced that Linfield had lost, the dog went berserk.
'What's up with the dog?' asked the barman.
'He's a Linfield fan,' explained the man. 'He always goes wild when they get beat.'
'What does he do when they win?'
'I don't know – I've only had him ten months.'

What about the Irishman in a bedding factory who asked for a week's lying time?

During a drought in the Republic, the groundsman of a shinty club came up with an idea to make the water go further. 'Let's dilute it,' he suggested.

☆

Tough on the Kerry man who bought a second-hand car which had only one previous owner. It turned out to be the Dukes of Hazzard.

☆

Magnus: 'What's a Hindu?'
Patrick: 'Lay eggs.'

'You look tired, Sean.'
'Sure I'm always the same when I travel with my back to the engine.'
'Why didn't you ask the person opposite to change places?'
'I would have – but there was no one there.'

Then there was the Irish film star who did all his own stunts. They had to use a stand-in for the acting parts.

A Dublin student was asked by his teacher to read the phrase 'Where are you going?' with more expression, 'not forgetting that little thing at the end of the sentence.'
This time he said: 'Where are you going ... *little fishhook looking thing?*'

'I hear you're not going to Venice this summer, Bridget?'
'No, that was last year. This year we're not going to Rome.'

Definition of an Irish intellectual: someone who can listen to the *William Tell Overture* without thinking of *The Lone Ranger.*

101

A priest and a rabbi were bitter enemies. When the priest bought a new car, the rabbi did the same.
Then the rabbi watched in consternation as the priest sprinkled holy water on the bonnet of his car and blessed it.
After some thought, the rabbi went to the back of *his* car and sawed five inches off the exhaust pipe.

Notice in an Irish church hall: Keep-fit classes are cancelled due to illness.

Two Irishmen going into a cinema were followed down the aisle by an usherette with a torch.
'Watch out,' warned one, 'here comes a bicycle.'

Michael bought a young dog, but it wouldn't stop barking so he took it to a vet. The vet took one look at the dog and kicked it, whereupon it shut up.
'That's marvellous,' said Michael. 'How did you do it?'
'Easy,' replied the vet, 'Hush Puppies.'

Did you hear about the Irish bus conductor who went to work in a turban so he would get Sikh pay?

'Tell me, Sean, how is it you can teach your dog all those tricks and I can't teach my dog anything at all?'
'Well,' replied Sean, 'to begin with you've got to know more than your dog ...'

How many ears has the Irish Davy Crockett?
Three – a right ear, a left ear, and a wild frontier.

Card in a Galway shop window: 'Furnished room wanted in quiet house with ample cupboard space for elderly lady.'

Most Irishmen don't believe in the Blarney Stone. There are too many shamrocks around.

Eamonn went to his local pub for a game of darts. During the evening he met an attractive girl and went back to her flat, taking a piece of chalk with him.
When he finally arrived home his wife, spotting the chalk behind his ear, asked, 'Where have you been until this time of night?'
'If you must know,' replied Eamonn, 'I've been out with a woman.'
'Like hell you have,' exclaimed the wife. 'You've been playing bloody darts again!'

'You can't park your car here, Paddy,' said the policeman.
'Why not?'
'You're on my foot.'

☆

Irish graffiti: SAVE ENERGY, DON'T MOVE.

☆

An Irish farmer took his wife out to celebrate their golden wedding. In the restaurant he ordered a bottle of champagne.
The waiter duly produced it in a bucket of ice.
'What's the matter?' asked the farmer. 'Is the bottle leaking?'

☆

'Molloy,' said Lady Penelope, 'take off my coat.'
'Yes, my lady,' said Molloy.
'Now, Molloy, take off my dress.'
'Very well, m'lady,' said Molloy blushing.
'And don't let me catch you wearing my clothing again!'

☆

Pat limped up to the building foreman at the end of his first day of back-breaking work. 'Are you sure you've got my name right?' he asked.
'Yes,' said the foreman. 'Sean Simpson, isn't it?'
'Thank heaven – I thought you had me down as Samson.'

☆

The university cricket team was a man short, so they decided to enlist Sean the milkman. 'He's a marvellous bowler,' said the captain, 'just as long as he doesn't speak to anyone.'

So they rigged Sean out in the university colours and he took eight wickets for ten runs, which gave his team a resounding victory.

Later, in the bar, the rival captain congratulated him on his terrific performance. 'By the way,' he asked, 'what are you studying at university?'

And Sean, thinking quickly, replied brightly: 'Sums!'

An Irish farmer crossed a parrot with a hen, and bred a bird that comes and tells him when it's laid an egg.

Wife to depressed husband, 'What do you mean you have nothing to live for, Dominic? The house isn't paid for, the car isn't paid for, the washing machine isn't paid for, the television isn't paid for ...'

'What a lovely idea,' said Bridget to her new hubby, 'they've started printing our bank statement in red!'

Only an Irishman could invent oven-ready ice-cream.

A man rushed into the *Irish Times* office, and said excitedly, 'Quick, I want to put a notice in the paper. After ten years my wife's just given birth to a fine baby boy!'

'Congratulations, sir,' said the clerk. 'How many insertions?'

'Oh,' comes the reply, 'we lost count – hundreds!'

'Before I was nicked, I was makin' big money.'
'What happened?'
'I made it a tenth of an inch too big.'

Did you hear about the Cork man who was arrested for throwing Domestos at the Archbishop?
He was charged with bleach of the priest.

'The fact that the man was on his hands and knees in the middle of the road doesn't prove he was intoxicated,' argued the lawyer.
'Agreed,' said the policeman, 'but this chap was trying to roll up the white line.'

Then there was the Irish Olympic champion who had his gold medal bronzed.

Irish brickie: 'I'd like to work here, but there's no place to park my car.'
Foreman: 'I reckon you won't do then. We only hire brickies with chauffeurs.'

A Cork man came up with a perfect cure for headaches and depression. Divorce.

☆

Murphy took karate lessons, so he could kill a man with his bare feet. On his way home one night he was mugged. But by the time he got his shoes and socks off ...

☆

'How much longer are you going to be, Mary?'
'I've been tellin' you for over an hour – I'll be ready in a minute!'

☆

A lecturer was explaining to Seamus how nature sometimes compensates for a person's deficiencies.
'For example,' he said, 'if a man is deaf he may have keener sight. And if he's blind, then he may have a very keen sense of smell.'
'I see what you mean,' said Seamus. 'I've noticed that if a man has one short leg the other is always a bit longer.'

☆

Sign in a Letterkenny shop: 'We are open 24 hours a day, longer at weekends.'

☆

Then there was the Irish restaurant that advertised a seven-course dinner for under five pounds. A boiled potato and a six-pack of Guinness.

☆

A visitor to a Dublin hotel asked for an early call. When his phone went, the receptionist asked: 'Was it six or seven o'clock you wanted a call?'
'Actually, it was eight o'clock. What time is it now?'
'Ten forty-five.'

Two Irishmen in a café spotted a sign saying: 'Sorry, you can't eat your own sandwiches in here.' So they swopped theirs.

'What do you mean, Moloney, comin' home half drunk?'
'I ran out of money.'

In support of a pay claim, Irish wall-of-death riders have started a go-slow. – *News item*.

O'Shaughnessy beckoned over the nun who had been caring for him in hospital and said, 'Bless you, sister, and may all your sons be bishops.'

Foreman: 'You know you shouldn't smoke when you're working.'
Pat: 'Who's working?'

Irish Television bought twenty-six episodes of *Pot Black* under the impression it was a cooking programme.

How do they solve traffic problems in the Irish Republic?
There's a special lane for traffic jams.

'Waiter, have you any asparagus tips?'
'Sorry, sir – only Benson and Hedges.'

Irish package tour holiday: twenty-three days and four nights.

Definition of an optimist: An Irishman falling from the eighteenth floor of a building and shouting 'So far so good' at the tenth.

A priest was walking through Dublin, when one of his sandal straps broke. Seeing a shoemaker's sign 'Cohen and Son', he decided to further religious unity by letting the shop repair his strap.
A few days later Kelly the butcher was amazed to see a newly painted sign at the shoemaker's saying: 'Cobblers to the Priest.'
That afternoon a new sign appeared in Kelly's own window. 'Knackers to the Chief Rabbi.'

Said the Dublin hospital patient on receiving a hefty bill for a private operation: 'No wonder they all wore masks in the operating theatre!'

Magnus: 'Name two pronouns.'
Patrick: 'Who? Me?'

☆

A young Kerry man was hired by a supermarket. 'Your first job,' said the manager, 'is to sweep out the store.'
'But I'm a university graduate.'
'In that case, hand me the broom and I'll show you how.'

☆

Bridget was called up for jury service. 'What is your occupation?' she was asked.
'Housewife.'
'Any children?'
'Thirteen.'
'Your husband's occupation?'
'Manufacturer.'

☆

Then there was the wealthy Irish bachelor who advertised for a daily woman ... and hired all 365 of them.

☆

'Quickly, doctor, can you deal with an emergency?'
'I'm sorry I can't.'
'Please yourself ... your waiting room's on fire.'

☆

A Howth man was making an obscene phone call: 'I'll be coming up to your flat tonight when your husband's out, and I'll be taking off all your clothes *... and will you stop telling me the time when I'm talkin' to you?'*

Patient: 'You pulled out the wrong tooth.'
Dentist: 'Keep calm ... I'm coming to it.'

What about the Irishman who applied for a job at the Winter Olympics – gritting the Cresta Run.

Paddy's bi-sexual. If he can't get it, he buys it.

Then there was the grand reunion dinner in the Europa Hotel, Belfast, for the two thousand men who fought in Wellingtons.

Instructions on packet of Irish headache powder: 'Dissolve in water one hour before pain starts.'

'Many thanks for the £100 cheque for our old folks' fund, Mr Gilhooley, but you haven't signed it.'
'I know – I prefer to remain anonymous.'

The Irish hunter met a naked girl in the jungle.
'Are you game?' he asked.
'Yes,' she replied.
So he shot her.

Paddy to mate on building site: 'We'd better wear feathers on our heads tomorrow.'
'What on earth for?'
'I overheard the gaffer saying he was going to pay off all the cowboys tomorrow.'

Bridget got rid of her fridge. As she explained, it was too much trouble cutting ice into those little squares to fit the tray.

Doctor: 'I'm afraid you've got double pneumonia.'
Mike: 'Is that good for two prescriptions?'

Graffiti: DOUBLE YOUR MONEY – FOLD IT IN HALF.

Did you hear about the Irishman who opened a boomerang factory? He heard the sport was making a comeback.

Bridget wanted an animal-skin coat for her birthday ... so Sean bought her a donkey jacket.

'Look, Mr Delaney,' said the hotel clerk, 'I've told you a dozen times we haven't any rooms. We're full.'

'If the Prime Minister came in, you'd have a room for him, wouldn't you?'

'Why, of course.'

'Then let me have his room. He's not coming.'

Mrs Murphy was at her husband's wake. A friend came up, stood beside the coffin, and remarked, 'My, doesn't he look wonderful?'

'So he ought to,' came the reply. 'He's been jogging twenty-five miles a day.'

Then there was the Larne man who on his fiftieth birthday half expected a telegram from the Queen.

Bridget met her future husband in the Tunnel of Love. He was digging it.

A motorist was driving in Galway when his car suddenly stopped. As he got out to check the engine, an old horse trotted past and said, 'Try the spark plugs.'

The startled motorist went to a nearby farm house and told the farmer what had happened.

'Did the horse have a floppy ear?' asked the farmer.

'Yes,' agreed the driver.

'Well, don't pay any attention to him. He doesn't know a lot about cars.'

What about the Irish burglar who went to prison because of his belief? He believed the burglar alarm had been disconnected.

☆

'If you don't love your husband, Mary, why did you have nine children by him?'
'I tried to lose him in the crowd.'

☆

Sign in a shop window in Cork: 'Sale of conditioned cookers starts Friday. Can't last.'

☆

Then there was the Irish pop singer who got a platinum record for having a million copies of his latest disc – returned.

☆

A drunkard stopped a taxi and asked the driver, 'Do you know Galway Bay?'
'I certainly do,' replied the driver.
'Well, sing us a couple of verses.'

☆

'And at eight p.m. Eamonn Andrews says those three famous words: *This Is Your Life*.' – Irish paper.

☆

Pat checked his football coupon and found he had eight draws. 'Did you put an X for no publicity?' asked his wife.
'Sure, I did better than that,' Pat replied. 'I put him next door's name on it.'

☆

Not forgetting the Kerry man who thought High Cholestorol was a religious holiday.

☆

'Don't come down the ladder, Mick – I've taken it away.'

☆

'How much are your flowers?'
'A pound or fiftypence a bunch.'
'I'll have a fifty pence bunch.'
'Sorry, I don't have any left. But I can split a pound bunch for you.'
'That's fine.'
'Do you want the petals or the stems?'

☆

Pat in shoe shop: 'Do you sell wellies?'
'We certainly do.'
'Good – I'll have two.'

☆

What about the Irish spy ship off the Russian coast – secretly trawling for fish?

☆

'House and shop for quick sale. Tenant under notice to expire at end of November.' – *Irish paper.*

☆

A Belfast woman visited a neighbour who was a chronic borrower. Later she said that she felt more at home there than she did in her own house.

'I fell off a 60ft ladder yesterday, Pat.'
'Were you hurt?'
'No – I only fell off the first rung.'

The foreman ordered O'Malley to dig a hole eight feet deep. Later, he explained a mistake had been made, and ordered him to fill it up again.
O'Malley did so, but couldn't get all the dirt back into the hole.
'Typical,' snorted the foreman. 'You'll just have to dig that hole deeper.'

Sergeant: 'Go and stand at the end of the line, Murphy.'
'I can't, sarge, there's someone there already.'

Graffiti in a monastery. O ROSARY, I LOVE YOU.

'Do you want today's *Irish Times* or yesterday's?'
'Today's.'
'Then come back tomorrow.'

Trust an Irishman to invent a motor-bike roof rack.

'What are you doin' with all those windows, Eamonn?'
'What do you think? I've been window shopping.'

Mary to bank manager: 'If I open a joint account, how much will you put in it?'

☆

A Limerick boy on holiday wrote home to his mother that it was 106 degrees in the shade. His mother wrote back, 'Then keep out of the shade.'

☆

Brendan, a ninety-eight pound weakling, sent away for a set of barbells. After a few weeks a friend asked him how he was getting on.
'Fine,' he replied. 'I can lift them bars without too much trouble. Next month, I'm goin' to start putting the round things on the end of them.'

☆

Psychiatrist: 'Do you think you're cured of being indecisive, Mr Muldoon?'
'Well, doctor, I'm ... er ... not so sure.'

☆

'I hear the Allied Irish Bank is looking for a cashier.'
'But didn't they hire one just a month ago?'
'That's right – he's the one they're looking for.'

☆

What about the Irishman at the Job Centre who turned down a vacancy at the Eagle Laundry? He explained he'd never in his life washed an eagle.

☆

'Michael's in bed with a case of amnesia.'
'What did he put it in a case for?'
'He's forgotten.'

☆

It could only happen in Ireland. A newspaper published the headline, 'Half the Council are crooks' but was asked to retract it.
The following week it ran the heading: 'Half the Council are *not* crooks.'

☆

'Are you looking for a job, Murphy?'
'That I am.'
'Can you work with a wheelbarrow?'
'Oh, no – I know nothin' about machinery.'

☆

Then there was the Irishman who kept racing pigeons. But he never caught one.

☆

'Why wasn't I given a middle name, Dad?'
'Sure, son, when you were born we couldn't afford that kind of luxury.'

☆

After Pat put in a flagstone walk from the house to the street, he called his wife for a look.
'That's terrible,' she said. 'The colours don't match, it's too narrow, and the stones are crooked.'
'Tell me,' asked Pat, 'how is it for length?'

☆

'Why did your wife stop helpin' you with the ploughing, Dan?'
'She said the harness was hurtin' her shoulders.'

☆

The Irish Space Agency have invented a convertible capsule so their astronauts can ride with the top down if the weather's fine. – *News item.*

☆

Pat was out driving, when his wife said she fancied a cup of tea. So he pulled in at a 'T' junction.

☆

Sign seen during a Dublin beer strike: 'Don't waste time going to your pub – it's pintless.'

☆

Spare a thought for the two would-be Irish bank robbers. They were caught stealing the stockings to wear as masks.

☆

Irish street sign: 'Waiting limited to sixty minutes in every hour.'

☆

Sign in a Co. Kildare churchyard: 'As maintenance costs are rising every month, members are asked to kindly cut the grass around their own graves.'

☆

'This match won't light, Mike.'
'What's the matter with it?'
'Search me – it was all right a minute ago.'

☆

Mulligan believes so strongly in reincarnation that he's made a will leaving everything to himself.

A Belfast trader was asked for 'a pair of men's trunks with legs in them'.

☆

Definition of bad luck: an Irishman breaking his leg in an Ear, Nose and Throat Hospital.

☆

Wife: 'I've some good news for you, Anthony.'
Husband: 'What's that?'
Wife: 'You haven't been paying those car insurance premiums all these years for nothing!'

☆

'Are you the barber who cut my hair last time?' asked the Irish rock 'n' roll singer.
'It couldn't have been me,' he replied. 'I've only been here ten months.'

☆

Paddy was walking along the beams of a building under construction high above the street, while pneumatic drills and compressors set up a nerve-jangling racket.
When he came down, a man who had been watching said admiringly: 'I was amazed at your calmness up there. How did you manage it?'
'Well,' came the reply, 'I used to drive a school bus, but I lost my nerve.'

☆

Mike discovered how to hammer nails without hitting his thumb. He got his wife to hold the nails.

☆

'What am I supposed to do with this?' grumbled driver Sean, as the traffic warden gave him a ticket. 'Keep it,' said the warden. 'When you get four, you receive a bicycle.'

☆

Then there was the Irishman who thought Bandaid was a musicians' charity.

☆

'Ma, I don't like cheese with holes in it.'
'Well, eat the cheese and leave the holes on the side of your plate.'

☆

Irish graffiti: I CAN'T SEE THE POINT OF DECIMALS.

☆

Then there was the Irish burglar who broke into a music shop and got clean away with the lute.

☆

When Michael told his wife he was thinking of getting a wig, she told him to try and get one with a built-in brain.

☆

A pity they had to cancel the Irish Boat Race. The course was waterlogged.

☆

Then there were the two Irish football teams in the Cup Final who decided to take the penalty kicks first.

A.L.O.I.J.B.—7

Pat and Mike were playing bingo.

'All the sevens – seventy-seven,' said the caller.

'Look, you've got that one,' said Pat.

'Four and nine, forty-nine,' continued the caller.

'You've got that one as well,' cried Pat.

'Look,' said Mike, 'would you mind keeping your eyes on your own card?'

'I can't,' replied Pat, 'I haven't any spaces left!'

Asked Bridget at the wake: 'And what did your poor husband die of, Mrs O'Connell?'

'Gangrene it was,' sobbed the widow.

'Well,' sighed Bridget, 'thank God for the colour of it, anyway.'

There was a record number of births in Liverpool last week. Apparently, it was all due to the Irish Sweep. But he's moved back to Dublin now.

'Did you know that deep breathing kills germs, Michael?'

'Yes, but how do you get them to breathe deeply?'

After Dennis had been inside for a year, his wife wrote, saying, 'There's no one to dig the back garden, so I'll have to do it myself.'

But he replied, warning her, 'Don't dig up the back. That's where I buried the haul.'

Soon he got another letter from his wife: 'What a to-do. Twenty coppers came round and dug up the entire back garden.'

'Right,' wrote Dennis, 'now plant the spuds.'

Then there was the Kerry man who played dominoes at Las Vegas, where all the diamond spots are real diamonds. He stole the double blank.

☆

Not forgetting the Irish traffic warden who ticketed two hundred cars at the Motor Show.

☆

'How's Barney getting on these days?'
'He was livin' the life of Riley — till Riley came home.'

☆

A man went into a Chinese restaurant in Killarney.
'Do you do takeaways?' he asked.
'Yes,' replied the waiter. 'Four from ten is six.'

☆

Two members of an Irish town council were berating each other. 'You're the biggest idiot in the world,' one shouted.
'And you're the most bigoted and prejudiced ass in the town,' yelled the other.
'Quiet, gentlemen, please,' interrupted the chairman. 'In your excitement, you seem to have forgotten that I am in the room.'

☆

A travelling salesman knocked on the door of a boarding house in Larne. 'Do you take lodgers?' he asked.
'That depends,' came the reply. 'Which lodge do you belong to?'

☆

Then there was the Irishman who bought his wife a present for their pearl wedding. A pearl electric light bulb.

☆

Graffiti: 'I'VE JUST BEEN MADE A PRIEST – CAN I GO OUT AND CELIBATE?'

☆

Sean went to his doctor for a checkup. 'You need exercise,' said the doctor. 'I want you to run fifteen miles every day.'
Three weeks later, the patient phoned the doctor to say he felt a lot better.
'Good,' said the doctor, 'but I'd like to give you another check. Come in this afternoon at 2.30.'
'I can't,' came the reply. 'I'm three hundred miles away.'

☆

Then there was the Limerick woman who didn't know her husband drank – until one night he came home sober.

☆

Not forgetting the Dublin man who was killed by drink. He was knocked down by a Guinness lorry.

☆

'How did you get on at the building society, Pat?'
'Not bad at all. They gave me a wheelbarrow, bricks, and a bag of cement.'

Pat and Mick went into business as tunnellers, and decided to put in a bid for the Channel Tunnel project.

Since their tender was easily the lowest, they were asked by an official to explain how they would go about tackling the job.

'Well,' said Pat, 'I'll start diggin' from Dover, and Mick here will start diggin' from Calais.'

'And what happens,' asked the official, 'if you don't meet up?'

'In that case,' replied Pat, 'You'll get two tunnels for the price of one.'

Seamus asked the bank manager: 'What exactly is a personal loan?'

Replied the manager: 'It's like this. As long as you keep up the payments – fine.'

'What if I don't?'

'That's when we get personal.'

'I'm afraid, Mr Shaughnessy,' said the doctor, 'you've only got two weeks to live.'

'In that case, doctor, can I have the last week in July and the first week in August?'

Then there was the Kerry man who said his house had solar heating. No roof.

A salesman spent two hours trying to sell Eamonn a lawnmower. 'Your neighbour has bought one,' he said in desperation.

'In that case,' remarked Eamonn I ll borrow his.'

☆

What about the Irishman who asked his butcher, 'Give us a sheep's head ... and cut it as close to the tail as you can.'

☆

Dan (in hospital bed): 'I've had my appendix out.'
Fellow patient: 'Have you a scar?'
Dan: 'No, I don't smoke.'

☆

Bus conductor: 'John Street ... Adam Road ... Mary Crescent ... Arthur Road ... James Avenue ...'
Michael: 'Isn't it time we got off?'
Patrick: 'Sit tight until your name's called.'

☆

'Waiter, there's a centipede in my soup.'
'Yes sorr, you see, we've gone metric.'

☆

Then there was the Limerick husband whose wife made him instant pudding. He got instant indigestion.

☆

'A pity about Mary. Remember she had a detached retinue?'
'Indeed, so I do.'
'Now I hear she's got a cyst on her aviary.'

☆

Doctor: 'What seems to be the trouble, Mrs Docherty?'
'It's my husband, Frank, doctor. He keeps thinkin' he's a TV aerial.'
'Give him these pills. They should cure him.'
'I don't want to cure him – I want you to adjust him so I can get Channel Four.'

☆

Sean to lawyer: 'I'd like you to sue that man across the road.'
'On what grounds?'
'He called me a warthog six years ago.'
'Six years ago? Why have you waited so long?'
'I went to the zoo today, and I saw a warthog for the first time.'

☆

'I mended that hole in your pocket after you went to bed, Brian.'
'Thanks ... but tell me one thing – how did you discover I had a hole in the first place?'

☆

Irish gravediggers went on strike today, but will still handle emergencies. – *News item.*

☆

'What's the trouble, Sam?'
'I've got seenus trouble.'
'Don't you mean sinus?'
'No – I was out with Murphy's wife and he *seenus*!'

☆

How about the pensioners on a bus mystery tour who had a sweep on where they were going? The driver won fifty-seven pounds.

Then there was the Irish singer called Wells Fargo. Mind you, that was his stage name.

A fire engine went whizzing up an Irish street, its siren screaming. A drunk staggered after it, chased it a mile, then finally collapsed in a heap. 'All right,' he sobbed, *stuff your ice lollies!*'

'I can always tell when my husband's lying to me, Bridget.'
'How can you do that?'
'Easy. I look in his eyes, then I look at his lips. If his lips are moving, he's lying.'

Irish graffiti: SAVE PETROL, MAKE ROADS SHORTER.

☆

'I thought you said you had a job as a liftman, Sean?'
'So I did, but I kept forgetting the route.'

☆

Driver to Irish garage attendant: 'Would you mind checking my tyres?'
'Certainly, sir. Yes, all four of them are there, all right.'

☆

An Irish man turned up at a fancy dress party in a smock, carrying a crook, and with a straw in his mouth. 'I'm a spy,' he told the hostess.

'A spy – dressed like that?' she asked.

'Yes,' came the reply, 'I'm a shepherd's spy.'

☆

Pat: 'I thought you were making beans on toast?'

Mary: 'So I was, but I can't get the beans out of the toaster.'

☆

'Good news,' said Desmond. 'I've found a great job. Good pay, a four-day week, and six weeks holiday a year.'

'Wonderful,' said his wife. 'What's the catch?'

'You start next Monday.'

☆

Then there was the Irishman who thought Grecian 2000 was Ronald Reagan's 'phone number.

☆

A Belfast mechanic made his own car from the wheels of a Granada, a Metro radiator, a Cavalier engine, a Renault body and the transmission from a Jaguar. Guess what he ended up with? Five years.

☆

Confusing for the ten daughters and ten sons of a mother in the Republic. They didn't know if she was a good Catholic or a sloppy Protestant.

What about the Irishman who had a candlelit dinner with his wife? The Gas Board cut him off.

Pat and Mick were called up for the Army. Said Pat: 'I'm going to fool them. I had a hernia once, so I'm going to wear my truss.'
Three doctors examined him, and put down 'ME' – 'Medically Exempt'.
When it was Mick's turn, he borrowed Pat's truss and went off to the draft board. The same three doctors examined him, and again put down 'ME'.
'Medically Exempt?' asked Mick.
'No – Middle East,' came the reply. 'Anyone who wears a truss upside down should have no difficulty riding a camel.'

Biblical note: It wasn't just Lot's wife who looked back and turned into a pillar of salt. Mulligan's wife looked back while driving and turned into a tree.

John got a job putting in telegraph poles. At the end of the first day, the foreman asked him how many poles he'd put in. 'Five,' replied John.
'That's not many,' said the foreman. 'Gerald over there has put in thirty-three.'
'Ah,' said John, 'but look how far his are sticking out of the ground.'

☆

'Do you have any African violets?' asked Kelly in the flower shop.

'I'm sorry, no,' came the reply, 'but we've some lovely potted geraniums.'

'No use,' said Kelly. 'It was an African violet I was supposed to water while she was away.'

Sean at Irish airline counter: 'I'll take two chances on your next flight to London.'

'Wellies for sale. Only worn once. From 7 February 1958 to 28 August, 1973.' – *Small ad*.

Irish shop steward: 'I vote that we only work on Tuesdays.'

Voice in crowd: 'What – *every* Tuesday?'

Then there was the Dublin road contractor who was offered a new Vauxhall Cavalier by a client as a goodwill gesture.

'I'm sorry,' said the contractor, 'the ethics of my job don't allow me to accept such a gift.'

'Very well,' said the client, 'suppose I was to sell you the car for £150?'

'That's different,' said the contractor. 'I'll take two.'

Spare a thought for the Kerry woman who wouldn't watch her TV on Friday because it's a Pye.

'Tell me – why are you driving on the pavement?'
'Well, it's like this, officer, I've no Road Tax.'

☆

A drunk walked into the War on Want office in Cork. 'Is this the War on Want place?' he asked.
'Yes, it is. What can I do for you?'
'It's like this – I've come to surrender.'

☆

A Scotsman, an Englishman and an Irishman were chatting about their health.
'If my doctor told me that I had only six months to live,' said the Englishman, 'I think I'd cash in everything I had and take a six months trip round the world. What would you do?'
Said the Scot: 'I'd buy a distillery, and drink the place dry.'
The Irishman considered, then said, 'I'd go and see another doctor.'

☆

Two Irishmen were in a cemetery looking at gravestones. 'Look,' said one, 'here's a stone that's 107 years old.'
'That's nothing,' said the other, 'this one's 159.'
'Whose is that?'
'I dunno – it just says "Miles to London".'

☆

A Galway driver, booked for drunken driving, complained that the police had made him take a sobriety test without giving him time to study for it.

☆

'What's the purpose of your short-term loan, Mr O'Grady?' asked the bank manager.
'It's like this,' came the reply, 'I just want something to tide me over till I can get some credit cards.'

Pat and Mick went fishing. 'What did you bring for lunch?' asked Pat.
'Ten six-packs of Guinness and half a packet of Jacobs' water biscuits,' came the reply.
'You're some man,' said Pat. 'Sure, what on earth do you expect to do with all those biscuits?'

'Listen to this,' said Kathleen. 'This woman in the paper was married four times, and each time her husband died she had him cremated.'
'Isn't that just like the thing?' said Mary. 'Here we're sittin' without husbands, and that woman has husbands to burn.'

Magnus: 'What's an albino?'
Patrick: 'An old comic.'

An English couple went to a Bray guest-house for a holiday, and found a swarm of bluebottles in the room.
'Good grief,' said the husband, 'the flies are really thick in here.'
'What do you expect?' asked the landlady. 'Open University ones?'

Note on a Dublin menu: 'The optional service charge is compulsory.'

A Scotsman, an Englishman and an Irishman went on a ten-day package cruise for £15 ... and found themselves adrift in a rowing boat in the Atlantic.
'We've been done,' said the Englishman. 'We've no oars. How will we get back?'
'Don't worry, Jimmy,' said the Scot, 'they'll send a helicopter for us.'
And the Irishman said, 'They didn't last year.'

A pity about the Irish runner who won the Olympic Marathon at Los Angeles. It was a false start.

'You know something, Pat? Your wife's two-faced.'
'Don't be daft – if she was she wouldn't wear that one.'

Two Irishmen were travelling by train from London to Glasgow, and one got out at every station, jumping on again at the last minute.
'What's the matter?' asked the other. 'Have you got kidney trouble? Sure, there's a toilet on the train.'
'It's not that,' came the reply. 'You see, my doctor says I've a very bad heart so I'm only booking from station to station.'

☆

A man selling the elixir of life at an Irish fair told the crowd: 'It'll restore your health ... put you on top of the world ... keep you from getting old. Look at me – would you believe I'm 105 years old?'

An onlooker asked the man's youthful assistant: 'Is he really 105?'

'I'm not sure,' came the reply. 'I've only been working for him for 77 years.'

'I thought the doctor told you to cut down on alcohol, Sean.'

'So he did.'

'Then what are you doing about it?'

'I've stopped the wife from drinking.'

Asked the priest: 'Do you believe in the Father the Son, and Holy Spirit?'

'Look, I've ten minutes to live, Father, and here you are asking me riddles!'

'So you wish to marry my daughter, Sean? Do you think you can support a family?'

'I t'ink I can. How many of you are there?'

A driver followed a motor-cyclist along the road. Every time they stopped at a traffic light, the motor-cyclist fell over.

Finally, the driver wound down the window and asked, 'How long have you been falling off your motor-bike?'

'Ever since I sold the sidecar,' came the reply.

☆

'You know, Michael, I never slept with my wife before we got married. How about you?'
'I couldn't say. What's her name?'

☆

Beware of a five-star hotel in Ireland. You can see them through the ceiling.

☆

'I thought you were going to write "Happy Birthday" on the cake, Kathleen?'
'So I was … but I couldn't get it into the typewriter.'

☆

Paddy: 'So you fancy yourself as a plumber. Where are your references?'
Sean: 'I left them at home.'
Paddy: 'You're hired.'

☆

Card in Kerry shop window: Will the person who took my ladder on Friday please return it or further steps will be taken.

☆

Why did the weatherman appear on Irish TV wearing one glove? He said it would be warm tomorrow … but, on the other hand, it might be cold.

☆

Talking of cold … the O'Reillys couldn't afford coal during the winter. So they all sat around an extra strong mint.

'You shouldn't have trodden on that spider and killed it, Mick – they're lucky.'
'That one wasn't.'

☆

A Panda car drew up in a street in Belfast ... and a Panda got out.

☆

Trust an Irishman to invent night storage solar panels.

☆

Notice in a Larne shop: 'Easy credit terms. Half down and the rest now.'

☆

A Scotsman, an Englishman and an Irishman were discussing what was the greatest invention.
'Without any doubt,' said the Englishman, 'the telephone is the greatest.'
'I don't agree,' said the Scot. 'For my money the television is tops.'
'In my opinion,' said the Irishman, 'the thermos flask beats the lot.'
'How do you make that out?' asked the Englishman.
'Well,' explained the Irishman, 'when you put something hot in a flask, it stays hot. If you put something cold in it, it stays cold. *How does it know?*'

☆

A pub in Ireland specialises in David and Goliath cocktails. One small one and you're stoned.

Still on drink, an Irishman in a pub knocked back fourteen whiskeys in eleven seconds.

'You don't half drink fast,' said an onlooker.

'I know,' came the reply. 'I had one knocked over once.'

Did you hear about the Cork man whose mother-in-law fell over the dog? He was on to the vet in a second.

In the Transatlantic single-handed yacht race, Brendan O'Reilly has been disqualified for using both hands. – *News flash*.

'Your £500,000 pools cheque will be presented to you at the Odeon tonight, Mr Kelly.'

'Couldn't you make it the Plaza? I've already seen the film at the Odeon.'

Then there was the drunkard who followed a water sprinkler down O'Connell Street to tell him his wagon was leaking.

And the Tipperary woman who got a job as a lollipop lady at Brands Hatch.

'I'm afraid we haven't enough money for a holiday, Bridget.'

'Yes, we have,' she contradicted him. 'Every time we made love, I put one pound in the bank.'

'Did you now?' said the husband. 'If only you'd told me, I'd have given you *all* my business.'

Car sticker in Dublin: BRAIN IN NEUTRAL.

'What did you buy for Maureen's birthday, Jack?'
'I got her a rocket.'
'A rocket? Was she pleased?'
'Not half – she was over the moon.'

Talking of birthdays, Seamus was given a dictionary for *his* birthday. He said that he couldn't follow the story, but at least each word was explained as he went along.

Why do Irish traffic wardens have yellow bands on their hats? So you won't park on their heads.

Then there was the Kerry man who thought a camp site was Danny La Rue in curlers.

Len applied for a job at a car factory. 'Can you brew tea?' he was asked.

'Yes,' he replied.

'Drive a stacker truck?'

'Yeah, but how big are the teapots?'

Schizophrenia is a big problem in Ireland. Two in one people have it.

Scrawled on a car driven by a lone man in Cork: JUST MARRIED.

'Did you know Bridget is getting married?'

'Married? I didn't even know she was pregnant!'

Michael was showing a friend a new, unloseable golf ball. 'If it goes in the rough,' he explained, 'it sends out a bleep. When it goes into the water it floats, and it glows in the dark.'

'That's amazing,' said his pal. 'Where did you get it?'

'I found it,' replied Michael.

Asked the magistrate: 'How many times have you appeared in this court for being drunk and disorderly, Murphy?'

'Sure, your honour, I thought *you* were keeping count!'

'What's a good thing for a hangover, Eamonn?'
'Drinkin' heavily the night before.'

☆

A Scotsman, an Englishman and an Irishman were discussing which animal they'd like to return to earth as.
'I'd like to come back as a giraffe,' said the Scotsman.
'I'd come back as a tiger,' said the Englishman.
'I'd choose to come back as a hyena,' said the Irishman.
'Why a hyena?' asked the other two.
'Well,' explained the Irishman, 'if you come back as a hyena, you're laughing!'

☆

'Knock Knock.'
'Who's there?'
'An Irish SAS man.'

How about the Irishman who got a job as a puppeteer by pulling a few strings?

☆

'I see they're puttin' VAT on fish and chips, Paddy.'
'Are they now? I still prefer them with vinegar.'

'What are you drinking, Sean?'
'I'll have a Bloody Alice.'
'Don't you mean a Bloody Mary?'
'No, a Bloody Alice – one drink and you're in Wonderland.'

☆

141

Notice outside a church in Co. Kerry: 'The preacher for next week will be pinned to the notice board.'

☆

'Geoffrey Boycott had his *bails* whipped off.' – *Irish news agency correction.*

☆

'About your double glazing, Mr Connolly, you haven't made any payments for three years.'
'That's perfectly true. But you told me it would pay for itself in twelve months.'

☆

Sad about the thirty Irish families evicted from Stonehenge. They thought it was a Barratt show house.

☆

'Doctor, I wake up laughing at myself.'
'I've told you before, Mr Kelly, you should wear pyjamas.'

☆

A couple from Connemara decided to try a mixed sauna, so they went along and stripped off. But when the steam cleared they found they were in a fish-and-chip shop ...

☆

News flash: Argentina has declared war on Ireland. They've taken the keys off the corned beef tins.

☆

A driver ran into a police station in Drogheda and shouted: 'Come quickly, sergeant – I've just hit a student.'
'Sorry, sir, it's Sunday,' replied the sergeant. 'You can't collect the reward till tomorrow.'

☆

Wife: 'I had to leave the car. There was water in the carburettor.'
Husband: 'Where is it now?'
Wife: 'In the Liffey.'

☆

An Irishman sent the Aga Khan one of Shergar's legs and demanded one million pounds 'or the horse won't race again'.

☆

Did you hear about the Cork driver who managed to get rid of a persistent noise in the back of his car? He let her sit in the front.

☆

Patrick: 'This cake is burnt. Did you make it according to the recipe?'
Mary: 'No – it's one of my own cremations.'

☆

Then there was the Irish typist who typed twenty-four letters in one day. Two more, and she would have completed the alphabet.

☆

'One-Armed Golf Title Changes Hands' – *Irish paper headline.*

☆

A Waterford motorist wanted to put his car in for a service ... but he couldn't get it through the chapel door.

☆

A burglar broke into a health shop in Killarney and stole the entire stock. Police are waiting to interview a man who lives to be 105.

☆

'How are you after your accident, Sean?'
'The doctor says I'm all right, but the lawyer says I still need the crutches.'

☆

Said Kathleen to Bridget at the disco: 'I'm forgetting boys tonight.'
'Me, too,' agreed Bridget. 'I'm for getting a couple as soon as we can.'

☆

Paddy was returning from a wedding with his wife and young son when he was stopped by the police and breathalysed. The test was positive.
'I'm afraid you'll have to come down to the station,' said the officer.
'Wait a minute,' protested Paddy. 'I haven't had a drink all day. Try the breathalyser on my ten-year-old son and see what happens.'
The officer did and again the test was positive. 'It looks as if the apparatus is faulty,' said the officer. 'You're free to go.'
As Paddy drove off, he remarked to his wife: 'I *told* you it was a good idea to give the boy a double whiskey before we left!'

☆

'Where did you learn to kiss like that, Dermot?'
'If you must know, I used to syphon petrol during the tanker drivers' strike.'

Sean phoned his wife from the pub to say he'd been delayed at the office.
'Don't give me that,' replied his wife. 'Get out of that boozer at once. This is a recorded announcement.'

'How did you guess it's a TV dinner?' asked Mary.
'Because it's repeating on me already,' he replied.

Bridget suggested her husband leave his body to science. 'That way it won't be completely wasted,' she explained.

Then there was the Dublin man who had had a cruise holiday each of the last three years, and on each occasion his wife got pregnant. This year he's taking his wife with him.

A man drove into a car wash. When he was through, the attendant took the money and said: 'Thanks a lot, Paddy.'
The driver was astonished. 'How did you know I was Irish?' he asked.
'Well,' explained the attendant, 'we don't get many motor-cyclists in here.'

☆

'It's a boy!' the doctor told Kevin. 'Eight pounds exactly.'
'Great,' said the flustered Kevin. 'Will you take a cheque?'

Three Irishmen in a taxi. When they arrived at their destination, the meter said 80p, and the driver asked for 90p to cover the third passenger.
'But it says only 80p on the meter,' protested one, 'and 80p is what you're going to get.'
'Yes,' said the other two, 'and that's all you're getting from us as well!'

Sean got a phone call from the blood bank – to say that his blood had bounced.

When the jury reassembled in a Dublin court, the judge noticed that one of the jurors was missing.
'I can explain that, your worship,' said the foreman.
'Mr Kilpatrick has gone off to the races – but he's left his verdict with me.'

'Take three teaspoonfuls of this medicine after every meal, Mrs Dougherty.'
'But, doctor, I've only got the two teaspoons.'

Notice in Irish furrier's: 'A small deposit secures any fur coat until your husband gives in.'

'Paddy, you're working very hard, carrying bricks up and down the ladder at that speed.'
'Not so loud. I have 'em fooled ... they're the same bricks all the time.'

☆

The phone rang in the legal offices of O'Brien, O'Brien, O'Brien and O'Brien. 'Hello, can I speak to Mr O'Brien, please?'
'Sorry, Mr O'Brien is in court.'
'Well, can I talk to Mr O'Brien?'
'Sorry, he's out of town.'
'Then put me through to Mr O'Brien.'
'He won't be back until three, I'm afraid.'
'All right – I'll speak to Mr O'Brien.'
'Speaking ...'

☆

Priest: 'I must ask you this, Mulligan. Have you ever had sex out of wedlock?' Mulligan: 'Not me, Father. I don't even know where the place is.'

☆

Then there was the Irish butcher who went to Stockholm for a sex change operation. It cost him £45,000 and left him without a sausage.

☆

P.S. He'd have been better having his operation in London. Just snip, snip, snip, and Bob's your Auntie!

☆

Still on operations, did you hear about the Ballymena man who had his toes amputated so he could get closer to the bar?

☆

Or the Dublin man who calls his wife Exocet?
Once she's on her way, there's no stopping her.

Sean likes it to be known he's a member of the jet
set. Well, he's a fitter with the Gas Board.

'What's this seafood diet you're on, Pat?'
'It's like this – when I see food, I eat it.'

Then there were the three Irishmen found by
Customs in a crate at Dublin Airport. They
explained they'd booked a package holiday to
Corfu.

Did you hear about the Cork architect in prison
who complained to the Governor that the walls
weren't built to scale?

'Yon Bridget's a witch and no mistake, Seamus.'
'How do you make that out, Michael?'
'She, I was driving along and I put a hand on her
knee and she turned into a lay-by.'

Then there was the Irish athlete who went into a
seafood restaurant and pulled a mussel.

And the tourist who asked the waiter: 'What are the prawns like today?'
Replied the waiter: 'Little pink fishes, same as yesterday.'

☆

How about the Donegal couple who called their son Six and Seven Eighths? They picked his name out of a hat.

☆

'Can I use your sledge, Pat?'
'Sure – we'll go halves.'
'Fantastic!'
'Yes – you can have it uphill and I'll have it downhill.'

☆

Spare a thought for the two Irish burglars who were all set to blow a safe when one of them ran out of puff.

☆

'Why did you call your daughter Onyx?'
'Well, you see, Mary, she was Onyx-pected.'

☆

A Killarney man answered an ad in a paper for light housework ... and got a job in a lighthouse.

☆

Patrick stopped outside the village blacksmith's. 'Come quick, Mike,' he shouted. 'There's a man here making a horse – he's just nailin' on the back feet!'

149

'Where did you get on the bus?' the inspector asked Seamus.

'Downstairs,' he said.

O'Reilly was walking his dog one evening, when he was stopped by a policeman. 'If I catch your dog fouling the pavement,' he warned, 'I'll take you in. Train him to go in the gutter.'

A few nights later, the policeman passed O'Reilly again. 'Where's your dog tonight?' he asked.

'He's dead,' replied O'Reilly.

'What happened?' asked the policeman.

'Well, I was training him to go in the gutter and he fell off the roof.'

An Irishman set out to cross the Atlantic on a plank. But he couldn't find one long enough.

Then there was the Lisburn man who gave his free-spending wife plastic surgery. He cut off her credit cards.

How about the Irish husband celebrating his jade wedding? He gave his wife a bottle of orangeade.

How about the Howth man who went to bed with a tape measure? He wanted to know how long he slept.

☆

It could only happen to an Irishman. He went to a mind-reader at Blackpool, and was charged half-price.

☆

Then there was the Irish burglar who gave his wife a fur coat and told her it was worth five years.

☆

'So you want a job, Murphy?' said the foreman. 'Tell me – are you a clock watcher?'
'Not really,' replied Murphy. 'I'm more of a hooter listener.'

☆

How about the Irish Setter that always sat on the stove? It thought it was a Range Rover.

☆

Sad about the Irishman in a Chinese restaurant who asked for Kung Fu instead of Egg Fu Yung and was kicked to death.

☆

Priest in pub: 'I'll have a Holy Mary.'
Barman: 'What's that?'
Priest: 'Vodka, without the tomato juice.'

☆

When Kevin was born, his father said it was a red letter day. He received final demands for the gas, electricity, and rates.

'You look a bit off colour, Kathleen.'
'Yes, I've a headache, a sore stomach, and a bad leg.'
'Why don't you go and see a doctor?'
'Sure, I will when I'm feeling better.'

☆

So many Irishmen have been involved in accidents with shooting sticks that the makers have put labels on them, 'This end in ground'.

☆

'Hey, Dermot, I've a pigeon that talks.'
'Get away – pigeons can't talk.'
'This one does – it speaks pigeon English.'

☆

Two Irishmen were at the Centre Court, Wimbledon. 'You know something,' said one, 'we've been here two hours and McEnroe hasn't taken a swipe at the umpire yet.'
'Just you wait until he comes down off that ladder,' the other replied.

☆

Irish TV Top Ten:
1. Dysentry.
2. Husky and Starch.
3. The Price Is Wrong.
4. This Is Your Wife.
5. Pan O'Rama.
6. News at a Quarter After Ten.
7. Pot Yellow.
8. It'll Be All Wrong on the Night.
9. The Sky at Noon.
10. Closed University.

☆

152

Diner: 'How do you get a glass of water in here?'
Irish waiter: 'Try settin' yourself on fire.'

☆

Then there was the man who got a couple of Irishmen to carpet his house from top to bottom. You can easily pick the house out — it's the one with wall-to-wall rubber.

☆

Did you hear about the Irish cat burglar who said in court he was politically motivated? He was a Meeowist.

☆

Not forgetting the cannibal who was converted by Irish Catholic missionaries. On Fridays he only eats fishermen.

☆

A man went into a Chinese restaurant and heard someone order lasagne.
'Lasagne ... in a Chinese restaurant?' he asked the waiter.
'Yes, sir,' came the reply. 'We try to please our Irish clientele.'

For years Gilligan and O'Mally had occupied neighbouring chalets for summer holidays, and Gilligan was feeling the monotony of it. So he suggested to O'Mally, 'Listen, I've an idea. How do you feel about swopping? We're lifelong friends, after all, and I expect you're a bit bored with your wife.'

'I must admit I've thought about that myself more than once,' O'Mally replied. 'Let's ask the ladies how they feel about it.'

So, very diplomatically, each consulted his wife and, to the delight of both husbands, they seemed agreeable. That night they swopped over.

Next morning, Gilligan asked O'Mally, 'How did you enjoy it?'

O'Mally beamed at the memory of the previous night. 'It was absolutely terrific,' he said. 'I think we should do it every night.'

'Those are my feelings exactly,' said Gilligan, 'Let's go next door and see how the girls got on.'

Irish proverb: A bird in the hand is useless if you want to blow your nose.

Did you hear about the Irishman who held up a bank? The gun was real, but he was a replica.

'I'm not saying Molly is the wrong side of forty, but the National Trust of Ireland looks after her beauty spot.'

'Tell me, Mr Gilhooly, are you still smoking?'
'Yes, doctor, but I'm down to ten a day.'
'Good – give me one, will you? I've left mine in the car.'

An Irishman was plummeting to earth from his plane when his parachute failed to open.
On the way down he passed another Irishman coming up.
'Do you know anything about parachutes?' asked the first.
'No,' came the reply. 'Do you know anything about gas ovens?'

A Lisburn man complained to the dole clerk that he couldn't find a job where he would not be required to work on Tuesdays.
'Why can't you work on Tuesdays?' asked the clerk.
'It's obvious, isn't it?' he replied. 'I come here on Tuesdays!'

☆

'Do you know anything about laying flagstones, Murphy?'
'I certainly do – I can lay them to a millionth of an inch.'
'That's no good to us. We've got to be spot on.'

☆

Asked the boss: 'What's your excuse for being late this time? And it better be good, Donnelly.'
'It is, it is,' his employee replied. 'I was run over by a marathon.'

How about the man in a Dublin restaurant who ordered a meal in French to impress everyone? Only it was a Chinese restaurant.

In the same restaurant some diners were having an argument. Finally, one of them called over a waiter and asked, 'Tell me something – do you have any Chinese Jews?'
'Very sorry,' he replied. 'Just pineapple juice, apple juice and orange juice.'

How about the Irishman flying to America who discovered he'd seen the in-flight movie? So he walked out half-way through.

Gravedigger wanted. Accommodation and incentive bonus. – *Irish paper.*

Why are there no Irish contestants in TV's *Film Buff of the Year*? They're too shy to take their clothes off.

A narrow escape for the Killarney man who tried out his wife's new washing machine. The paddles nearly beat him to death.

Did you hear about the fight in a Dublin chip shop? A lot of fish got battered.

Police are looking for an Irishman after a hold-up of an ice-cream van. The villain said 'Stick 'em up' – and grabbed the lolly.

☆

Doctor: 'I'm afraid, Mr Grogan, you've only got three minutes to live.'
'Is there nothing you can do for me, doctor?'
'Well, I could boil you an egg.'

☆

Irish station announcement: 'The train arriving at platforms 1, 2, 3, 4 and 5 is coming in sideways.'

☆

Then there was the witch who was a bit under the weather one day. But she managed to get up in the afternoon for a spell.

☆

Irish proverb: A friend in need is a friend to avoid.

☆

Sean mean? If you gave him poison, he wouldn't die till he'd recovered the deposit on the bottle.

☆

Notice in a Dungannon firm: The spare key to the first aid room is available in the first aid room.

☆

How do you make an Irish omelette? First, borrow six eggs.

☆

'What's your favourite drink, Pat?'
'The next wan.'

☆

An Irish policeman went to the doctor complaining of fatigue.
'I'll give you some pills and some advice,' said the doctor.
'What's the advice?' asked the policeman.
'Stop chasing getaway cars on foot.'

☆

Said the newly-wed bride: 'I've done you some cod that will melt in your mouth, Michael.'
'I've told you before – you've got to let it thaw out first!'

☆

Young Patrick got a part in a school play as a man who'd been married twenty years. Next time, he's been promised a speaking part.

☆

Then there was the Tipperary soldier on a camouflage course who couldn't locate the headquarters tent.

☆

Notice in a barber's shop window in Co. Clare: 'Home haircuts repaired.'

☆

A policeman in Waterford was detailed to watch for someone stealing undies from a clothes line. So he hid his bike in the bushes and moved off carefully round the area on foot.
He didn't catch the thief, but when he got back his bike had gone.

Notice in a Belfast launderette: 'This machine is permanently out of order.'

Irish proverb: If at first you don't succeed, give up.

Car sticker in Donegal: USE YOUR HEAD – IT'S THE LITTLE THINGS THAT COUNT!

Did you hear about the riot at Dublin's Mountjoy Prison? The Governor called in the Army and evicted the troublemakers.

Then there was the Aer Fungus charter excursion flight across the Atlantic. Instead of in-flight movies, they showed snapshots.

Cordon Bleu Cook wanted for government department dining room at Stormont. Good salary, excellent working conditions, bonuses, plus luncheon vouchers. – *Irish paper*.

Sean had quite a day at Dublin Zoo. He mugged an alligator and stole a handbag.

☆

1st kipper: 'They say smoking is bad for you.'
2nd kipper: 'That's all right – I've been cured.'

☆

Proverb: He who laughs last is an Irishman who hasn't seen the joke.